PRAISE FOR *BEYOND THE MIC DROP*

When people claim their stories, they claim their power. Melissa Jun Rowley illuminates how narrative becomes a force for human rights, dignity, and a future shaped by many voices—not imposed by a few.

—Peter Gabriel
Musician and human rights activist

Melissa's work reminds us that storytelling is key to building power for frontline communities, connecting real people to tangible solutions that benefit everyone. This book is the blueprint for strengthening movements and confronting the crisis of imagination.

—Rev. Lennox Yearwood Jr.
President and CEO, Hip Hop Caucus

Beyond the Mic Drop *is a must-read for climate activists and changemakers. It shows how transparency and accountability become transformative when people see themselves in the story and understand what is being risked, protected, and reclaimed—and it offers practical tools to change how we work, communicate, and act.*

—Catherine Atkin
Climate lawyer

In the environmental arena, I've seen how the stories we tell can either deepen inequities or spark transformation—and this book captures that truth with clarity and heart. Melissa Jun Rowley shows us that storytelling is a powerful tool for justice, belonging, and the systems change our communities and our planet urgently need.

—Radhika Fox
Former assistant administrator for Water,
US Environmental Protection Agency

In the beginning was the word. Without words, there would be no story. Humans are storytellers. In the age of creeping authoritarianism and oligarchy, there's never been a better time for a book to capture the story of this era.

—Mike Butcher
Founder and editor, Pathfounders;
former editor-at-large, TechCrunch

There has never been a more urgent time for this book. With our increasing inability to connect across differences, Rowley provides us the necessary tools to use narratives and storytelling to resolve conflict and build understanding.

—Susan McPherson
CEO, McPherson Strategies

Melissa Jun Rowley shows exactly why stories matter: to justice, to community, to our collective future, and to defending our democratic institutions. Beyond the Mic Drop *is riveting, urgent, and full of hope. As a teacher and storyteller myself, I'm deeply inspired by the work she's doing and the truths she's lifting up.*

—Sari Rosenberg
NYC Public School teacher and co-founder
of Teachers Unify to End Gun Violence

BEYOND THE MIC DROP

BEYOND THE MIC DROP

HOW OUR STORIES SHIFT CULTURE, POWER, AND POLICY

MELISSA JUN ROWLEY

Publish Your Purpose

Publish Your Purpose
141 Weston Street, #155
Hartford, CT, 06141

Ordering Information: Quantity sales and special discounts are available on quantity purchases by corporations, associations, and others. For details, contact the author at mel.rowley@gmail.com.

Edited by: Connie J. Mayse
Cover design by: Mark Pate
Typeset by: Medlar Publishing Solutions Pvt Ltd, India

ISBN: 979-8-88797-241-1 (hardcover)
ISBN: 979-8-88797-240-4 (paperback)
ISBN: 979-8-88797-242-8 (ebook)

Library of Congress Control Number: 2026904456

First edition, June 2026.

Publish Your Purpose is a hybrid publisher of nonfiction books. Our mission is to elevate the voices often excluded from traditional publishing. We intentionally seek out authors and storytellers with diverse backgrounds, life experiences, and unique perspectives to publish books that will make an impact in the world. Do you have a book idea you would like us to consider publishing? Please visit PublishYourPurpose.com for more information.

DEDICATION

For

my late father,

Carl Stedman Rowley,

who is still pushing me

higher on swings.

CONTENTS

ACKNOWLEDGMENTS

Writing this book was far from a solo act. The stories, ideas, and themes were inspired, challenged, and deepened by communities far and near by people whose missions, journeys, and belief in the power of story made every page possible.

To the team at PYP—Jenn T. Grace, Mina Lee, and Catherine Edens—thank you for your steady guidance throughout this process, shepherding this book from draft to completion. And to my copyeditor, Connie J. Mayse, and proofreader, Lily Capstick, thank you for your keen eyes and the care you brought to every page.

To my family who checked in on me religiously on how the writing was going during the weeks when it felt stuck and when it took over every corner of my mind, thank you for your patience, humor, and unwavering presence.

To the friends, colleagues, and collaborators who walked alongside me in conflict zones, on mountaintops, at climate summits, on stages, and through the quieter trenches of self-doubt, thank you for the courage of your own voices, for trusting me with your stories, and for reminding me to keep telling mine.

Some of the stories in this book were shared with great vulnerability. In chapter 11, names and identifying details have been changed to protect the privacy and safety of those involved.

To my teachers, guides, and fellow storytellers who have shown me that our most human narratives can become infrastructure for justice, freedom of expression, leadership, and democracy, thank you for your wisdom and generosity.

And to the readers, the dreamers, and the seekers of truth and beauty—the reason stories matter—thank you for being on this journey with me, for listening deeply, and for embracing your own power to create.

INTRODUCTION: A NOTE TO THE READER

Every culture is sustained by the stories it repeats. Every institution is reinforced by the stories it rewards. And every life is guided by the stories it accepts as true.

I've spent a large part of my life seeking and telling stories from across borders, literal and figurative. I've sat cross-legged on dusty floors in the Global South with women drafting business plans to create jobs for their local economies. I've walked through neighborhoods where murals and street art illustrated community identity so vibrantly that they gave rise to resistance, challenging government policies and dominant social narratives. I've interviewed remarkable humans sparking positive change in conflict regions, innovation hubs, and jungles. And through it all I've learned that stories are the bridges that survive when everything else falls apart.

What's become clear to me is that storytelling is more than a skillset, a craft, or a business strategy. It's a power, as my dear friend Sheryl Winarick would say.

This book traces that power in motion:

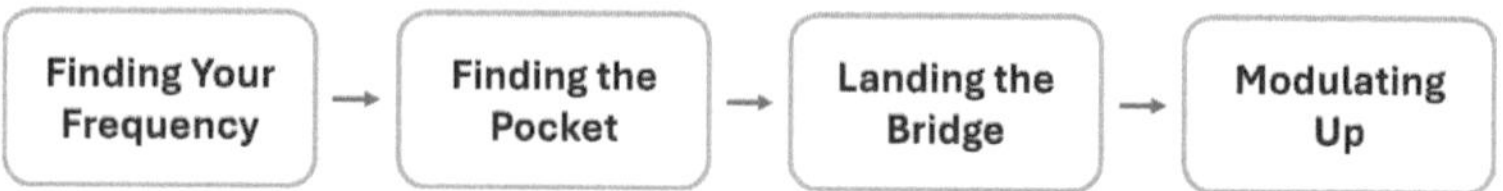

We begin by examining the narratives we carry. Then we explore how story can move across ideological, cultural, and political divides. Finally, we look forward to how storytelling drives leadership, technology, business, and legacy.

At the end of each chapter, you'll find mic checks, practices designed to help you work with your own stories. Write in the margins. Skip around. Return to what resonates.

You're already living inside stories about who you are, how the world works, what's possible, and what's not.

This book is an invitation to examine those stories with rigor and curiosity, to question where they came from, and to decide which ones you'll continue to live by and which ones you're ready to revise and claim in your own voice.

The pen and the mic are yours to grab.

Let's plug in.

PART 1

FINDING YOUR FREQUENCY

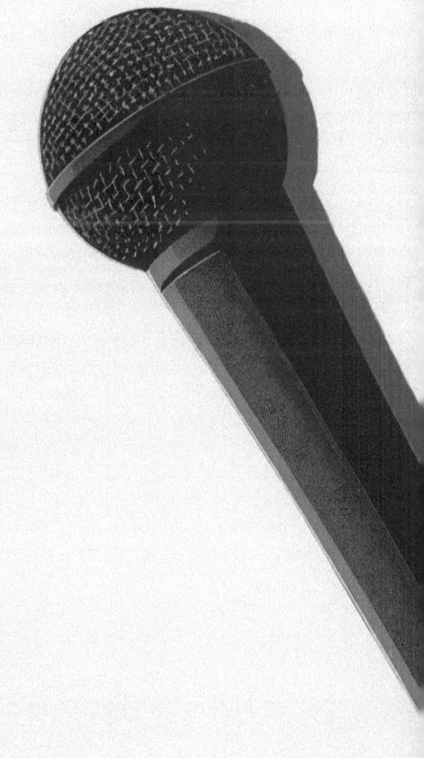

1

OWNING YOUR STORY MEANS OWNING YOUR POWER

We are all storytellers. We all live in a network of stories. There isn't a stronger connection between people than storytelling.

—Jimmy Neil Smith, founder, International Storytelling Center (ISC), Jonesborough, TN

We were speeding away from the one of the only bars in Los Angeles that played rock n' roll, pre-playlist era when the jukebox was still the hero. My cherry red Mustang convertible left a cluster of his swarming fans in the wake of what looked like a music-video casting call gone rogue.

Faces beaming with adrenaline called his name, reaching for a piece of him. My favorite David Bowie song, "Moonage Daydream," blasted from my car's speakers, as my hands clenched the wheel. I felt the thrill of racing through the back streets of Tinseltown with him in the passenger seat.

When I missed the turn to his house, I didn't think. I whipped the car into a hard, illegal U-turn. My tires squealed, and for a second it felt like the whole city tilted with us.

Finally, as soon as we hit a long stretch of road in East Los Angeles, away from traffic, he let out a low, gravely laugh.

"That was hot," he said, in the deep, scratchy voice that made him famous, though it landed softer in that moment.

"Good," I said. "I was a timid driver in high school. I got over that my first week living in New York City."

I paused, not sure if I wanted to take the conversation in a more serious direction. But then I went for it.

"How do you deal with that?" I asked. "With people all over you, wanting to take whatever percentage of you they can?"

He pulled out the bottle of whisky the bartender threw him before we ran out the door, and he took a long swig. "This is my life," he said before tilting his head back and closing his eyes, looking defeated and completely calm about the declaration he'd just made.

As if on cue, his phone erupted like an alarm that wouldn't stop, one call colliding into the next. His publicist called drilling with questions about why he'd slipped out of the event early. His manager buzzed, ticking off obligations for the next day like a metronome. A woman he met at the party purred into his voicemail, asking when they could get together and talk about a possible audition. The producer of his upcoming movie hammered on about call times and contracts. Each voice came out as if it was clawing at him. Each ring was a reminder that his body, his voice, and his hours weren't his own. It was less a life than a feeding frenzy, everyone around him circling ready to take a bite.

The wheels of my car continued to race, but everything inside of me went still. This is a story the public doesn't see, I thought to myself. They only see stories like the ones I had been assigned to cover earlier that day, the press junket for his latest film, the fame and glory. But behind every story and performance, there's a messier, beautifully human script—one written in shadows and silences. And there I was, sitting in it, watching the unedited version unfold.

"What am I doing?" I said out loud, almost forgetting he was sitting right next to me. It was more of an existential question about what I was doing with my life than about what was happening in that moment.

"You're giving me peace," he said. "Now keep driving east and don't get us killed."

The irony of him saying that beamed at me as bright as the stream of headlights rushing toward us. Cultivating peace, particularly inner peace, wasn't exactly my forte.

I used to thrive on the frequency of chaos. This was largely fed to me through people who were constantly on the run from their own reality. It was how I escaped my own stories, the ones that whispered all my flaws and shortcomings to me every chance they got.

Racing through that night was only the opening track. In the years that followed, I continued chasing the same high tempo experiences through different relationships, new continents, and temporary escapes.

For a while, the endless search was edifying and enchanting, and eventually became a part of my identity. I consistently encountered people whose lives opened windows into the kinds of realities I could never have grasped from books or the news. Each conversation carried a kind of unvarnished truth, and each country revealed layers of humanity I hadn't expected.

I was learning the ways of the world, and I was writing with a fierce commitment to telling stories that normally don't see the light of day.

But it wasn't until I learned to stay still and go inward, many years later, that I found my own voice. That's when this book began.

* * *

Looking back now, I can clearly see what was really happening when he and I sped away from Hollywood in my car, straight out of a TMZ video.

Later that night, in the cavernous privacy of his home that had no windows, only walls that seemed to echo back your own thoughts, I could hear how much he wanted to share the parts of him those fans could never touch—the scars, the insecurities, the hopes and anxieties, the truth of being human behind all the notoriety. I didn't know it then, but in that moment, my perception of storytelling, media, and influence was changing, and so was my idea of the kind of storyteller I wanted to be and the stories I wanted to tell.

Years later, when I found myself exploring start-up hubs and communities on the cusp of war zones, where peace felt more like a far-off whisper than a plan, I understood how and why that night altered my trajectory.

It wasn't just that the stakes were higher, though they were. What pulled me to parts of the world I never thought I'd roam was the chance to listen for the stories that revealed the wholeness of people, rather than the ones that reduced them to fragments. I'd begun to see how easily a narrative can be bent out of shape and how quickly people can be flattened into caricatures, villains, victims, or headlines, until the unique nuances of who they are disappear.

* * *

A decade after I raced through the streets of Los Angeles and transitioned from entertainment journalism to writing about human rights and climate action, I found myself in another speeding car, driving at the frequency of chaos. It was 2019. This time I was accompanied by new friends I had made in Tel-Aviv, four Israeli peace activists on a mission to help me understand Israel.

"If you want to understand Israel, you have to go to Palestine," said my friend Noam.

The next thing I knew we were driving through the desert, heading into the West Bank, even though the Waze app had just alerted us that we were entering an illegal zone for Israelis.[1] It was hailing hard in a freak storm that made the desert look almost haunted. Ice pelted the windshield as we barreled toward Ramallah.[2]

Inside the car, the energy was tense, yet tender. When we arrived at their Palestinian friend's house, the Palestinian and Israeli youth in the room shared that against all odds, hope for a two-state solution still lived in unlikely friendships across some parts of the region. The two older gentlemen who organized the meeting, one Israeli and one Palestinian, said they were no longer sure a two-state solution was possible. They'd seen and experienced too much. But I believe some semblance of hope still lived inside of them, if not for a two-state solution, then for the flickering possibility that friendship itself could outlast the ruins of politics. They were living proof of this.

I was sitting on the fault lines of history, listening as young people dared to imagine futures their elders stopped believing in

[1] Hunter Stuart, "Waze Lets Israelis Avoid Palestinian Areas, but Not the Other Way Around," *VICE Magazine*, October 5, 2016, https://www.vice.com/en/article/waze-lets-jewish-israelis-avoid-palestinian-areas-but-not-the-other-way-around/.

[2] Britannica Editors, "Ramallah," *Britannica*, October 23, 2025, https://www.britannica.com/place/Ramallah.

long ago. I felt humbled to be in that room at all. I was an outsider welcomed into their circle, chasing stories that my new friends believed might one day shift how entire communities across borders saw each other.

Those conversations hit differently now. I'm writing this in October 2025, as a ceasefire has taken hold in Gaza after years of war following the barbaric October 7 massacre in Israel. The scale of destruction, suffering, and loss is unlike anything I have witnessed in my lifetime.

As the world watches Israeli hostages returning to their families and Palestinian prisoners coming home, celebration fills the air. At the same time, many of us are wondering if or how long the ceasefire will last.

When I think of the day I drove into the West Bank and had the privilege of listening to an intergenerational group of people, who were born enemies, share their hopes and fears about the future, I can't help but ask, *What's the story the world is leaving behind as we watch this? When future generations look back, will they see only the rubble, the indifference, and the silence of those who had the power to intervene? Or will they also find evidence that amidst destruction, people insisted that entire lives not be reduced to numbers on a news ticker?*

The legacies we leave are formed not only by the actions we take, but by the stories we choose to amplify or ignore.

Beneath mountains of wreckage, rage, and the relentless cycle of retaliation, peace can feel impossible. Yet, the voices, stories, compassion, and grace of so many people I've met in the Middle East remind me that even when governments fail, people still find ways to hold on to one another's humanity. Their alliances have dared to cross borders that others declared a betrayal to their countries.

While this reflection doesn't erase the horrors of October 7 or the war in Gaza, it reminds us that another future is possible, and that stories, however small they may seem against the weight of history, remain one of the most vital tools we have to carve openings in the dark—tools that only exist because people insist on being heard.

Image 1. The Waze alert that appeared on my phone as we approached the West Bank.

WHAT WE'RE ALL AFTER

Behind every story lives the same longing to be understood. Because beyond ego and comparison, when our stories stay trapped inside us, they churn and claw. They wreak havoc on our souls, our loved ones, and our sleep patterns. And when voices are silenced by power, by fear, or by force, that pain doesn't live in private. It fractures entire societies.

This is happening now in front of our very eyes. Across headlines and algorithms, truth is being put on trial and silence is being sold as safety. In a moment like this, when freedom of expression is being dismantled by design, telling your story becomes more than an act of self-expression. It becomes an act of defiance and a declaration that your voice matters in a world trying to convince you it doesn't.

When you dare to speak fully, freely, and without apology, you're not simply living your own life. You're protecting the collective right to be heard, to question, to remember, and to imagine. Without this protection, cultures shrink, empathy erodes, and abusive power consolidates. A world without a plethora of diverse stories becomes a world run by a few.

On the most intimate level, silence can become a prison of our own making, because the stories we bury don't disappear; they harden inside of us. They become resentments, regrets, restless ghosts—the kind that show up at your door at 3 a.m. to remind you what you wanted to say deep down inside. And they never bring coffee or wine.

In a world so lined with control, silence is the sound of fear doing its job. Our stories serve as an interruption. They are the noise that refuses to fade, the spark that keeps the lights on when power cuts out, the jukebox in the corner that plays past closing time.

Even after the song fades, the frequency stays. Every voice has one, a note only it can hold. Some people call certain tones "noise."

My Dad used to call them all, whether sharp, flat, or somewhere in between, "a joyful sound."

FINDING YOUR FREQUENCY

By tuning into the pitch of your own truth and by letting it resonate without distortion or disguise, you become a ripple against deletion. And in a time when silence is being slammed onto us, that might be the most powerful stand you can take, because when stories are told from a place of integrity and vulnerability, they do more than move people; they stir culture. They ignite imagination. And they inspire the blueprints for systems and policies we haven't built yet.

Stories interrupt the status quo by humanizing what has been politicized and centering lived experience instead of theories.

In the West Bank, I listened as people long cast as enemies spoke to one another as neighbors. They talked about checkpoints and childhoods, land and loss. No one reduced the other to a slogan or a side. The labels that travel easily across headlines could not contain who they were in that space.

Conflict, in the abstract, is strategic and territorial. In a room like that, it's personal. It carries names, faces, trauma, and stubborn hope in the same breath. Once you witness those layers it becomes much harder to accept a version of the story that erases them.

That's why storytelling is so much more than self-expression. It's how we challenge dominant narratives and replace them with ones that reflect the competing realities of life. It's how we reimagine what's possible for ourselves, our communities, and the future we're trying to build.

This doesn't require a platform or a viral moment. It calls upon honesty and courage, and begins with telling the greatest, unending story we'll ever tell—our own—especially when it's the one that's hardest to speak aloud. That story emerges with attention to the memories and experiences that have stayed with you.

YOUR MIC CHECK

Mining for Gold

There is no greater agony than bearing
an untold story inside you.

—Maya Angelou

There are moments in your life you can return to with unsettling precision. You can recall the light in the room, the tone of a voice, and the weight of silence before someone spoke. Long after the details of ordinary days have faded, certain memories remain intact. They almost feel physical.

Psychologists call these *flashbulb memories*[3] when they're seared into us. These aren't just recollections of an event that happened. They entail the sensory details around the event. Think about the smell of a hospital corridor or the texture of the couch you sat on when the phone rang with bad news. The brain encodes emotionally charged experiences in the amygdala and hippocampus differently than neutral ones. That's why a fleeting glance, a gut instinct, or a moment you almost missed can live in you for decades.

---

[3] Roger Brown and James Kulik, "Flashbulb memories," *Cognition*, 5, no. 1 (1977): 73–99, https://doi.org/10.1016/0010-0277(77)90018-X.

The gold of a story isn't only in the grand, dramatic moments. It's also in the everyday instances your nervous system decided were essential, like the times you failed but kept going, when you were underestimated and still showed up, and when you made a choice that didn't change the circumstance, but changed you.

These moments form the raw material of your stories.

If those moments still live in you, they are asking to be examined. When you reflect on stories of your life that never seem to leave you, write down the following for your eyes only:

- Which memories arrive uninvited?
- Which details feel "lit up" in your nervous system?
- What silence in your life feels heavier than words?

TURN UP THE VOLUME

Once you've identified the memories that remain, the next step is to work with them deliberately. Here are five practices to raise your voice above the static, grounded in storycraft and psychology:

1. **Map the Moments**
   Sketch a rough timeline of your life and mark the memories that stayed. Neuroscience tells us emotional intensity predicts retention.[4] That's why you remember the sound of tires skidding

[4] Larry Cahill and James L. McGaugh, "Mechanisms of emotional arousal and lasting declarative memory," *Trends in Neurosciences*, 21, no. 7 (1998): 294–299, https://doi.org/10.1016/S0166-2236(97)01214-9.

during a near-accident but can't recall what you ate for lunch last Tuesday. Those moments are your emotional plot points. They're your roots.

2. **Find the Themes**

   When you step back, patterns emerge. Jung called these *archetypal motifs*.[5] They're the deep storylines our psyches circle again and again. Freedom. Belonging. Justice. Resilience. Psychologists studying narrative identity say people who recognize their personal themes report higher levels of meaning in life and resilience after hardship.[6] In other words, finding your themes isn't simply a literary exercise. It's psychological integration.

   These themes of belonging and agency become the emotional throughlines of our lives.

   Research in narrative psychology shows that people who can identify and make meaning from these recurring themes tend to report greater psychological well-being and resilience over time. In other words, noticing your patterns isn't simply reflective. It's integrative. It helps you understand how experience becomes identity.

3. **Speak from the Scar, Not the Wound**

   Trauma therapists warn against speaking from raw wounds too soon because doing so can reactivate the stress response. Scars, however, mark the place where healing has already begun.

---

[5] Carl G. Jung, *Man and His Symbols* (Aldus Books, 1964).

[6] Madhuri Ramasubramanian, et al., "The influence of life narrative themes on resilience and life outcomes," *Personality and Individual Differences*, 183, (2022): 111235, https://doi.org/10.1016/j.paid.2021.111235.

They carry perspective, not just pain. The act of retelling from a scar integrates memory into narrative, shifting it from the amygdala (emotional charge) into the prefrontal cortex (meaning-making).[7] That's why a heartbreak you once couldn't name can later be offered as a lesson in boundaries or self-worth.

4. **Ask the "So What?"**

   Psychologists studying narrative coherence emphasize the importance of *meaning-making*. A story doesn't need to be profound, but it does need a reason for being told. Ask the simple question of *So what?* Why does this matter, for you and for someone else? Even seemingly mundane stories like growing up in a house where no one said "I love you" can unlock recognition in another person. Your story becomes a mirror for someone else's identity, relieving isolation.

5. **Practice in Safe Places**

   Somatic psychology teaches us that the body is a truth-teller. Try your story first where you feel grounded. Journal it. Tell a trusted friend. Record yourself. Notice what happens in your body. Is there tightness in your chest or loosening of your breath? Those cues are data. They tell you whether your nervous system is ready to hold this story in public.

These practices are all ways of bringing your body, memory, and imagination into alignment.

[7] Elizabeth A. Phelps, "Human emotion and memory: interactions of the amygdala and hippocampal complex," *Current Opinion in Neurobiology*, 14, no. 2 (2004): 198–202, https://doi.org/10.1016/j.conb.2004.03.015.

THE DROP

Start small.
Start soft.
Start scared, even.
But start.

The moment you do, something subtle shifts. Your nervous system, once quelled by silence, begins to tune itself to courage. You're not only taking control of your own narrative. You're advocating for the collective rights of others to speak, to question, and to create.

Psychologist James Pennebaker found that writing or telling our stories, even privately, lowers stress, strengthens immunity, and clarifies thought.[8] Why?

Neuroscientists like Elizabeth Phelps and James McGaugh have shown that when emotion is translated into language the amygdala quiets and the prefrontal cortex lights up.[9] Storytelling literally

---

[8] James W. Pennebaker and S. K. Beall, "Confronting a traumatic event: Toward an understanding of inhibition and disease," *Journal of Abnormal Psychology*, 95, no. 3 (1986): 274–281, https://doi.org/10.1037/0021-843X.95.3.274.

James W. Pennebaker, "Writing About Emotional Experiences as a Therapeutic Process," *Psychological Science*, 8, no. 3 (1997): 162–166, https://doi.org/10.1111/j.1467-9280.1997.tb00403.x.

James W. Pennebaker and Joshua M. Smyth, *Opening Up by Writing It Down: How Expressive Writing Improves Health and Eases Emotional Pain (3rd ed.)* (Guilford Press, 2016).

[9] Phelps, "Human emotion and memory."

James L. McGaugh, "The amygdala modulates the consolidation of memories of emotionally arousing experiences," *Annual Review of Neuroscience*, 27, (2004): 1–28, https://doi.org/10.1146/annurev.neuro.27.070203.144157.

Matthew D. Lieberman, et al., "Putting Feelings into Words," *Psychological Science*, 18, no. 5 (2007): 421–428, https://doi.org/10.1111/j.1467-9280.2007.01916.x.

changes what the brain amplifies. It moves us from reaction to reflection, from survival to integration.

Every story you tell is a recalibration of the mind, the body, and the voice finding their shared frequency. It's how you come back into resonance with yourself after the world has tried to drown you out.

Culture changes the same way a synapse does, through repetition and relationship. One person speaks, another listens, and a bridge forms. Empathy travels across that bridge like a current, altering perception and even bias. This is how narrative becomes infrastructure for art and activism, as well as for healing, democracy, and belonging.

So write down a fragment of your story. Record it into your phone. Send it to a friend. Stand in front of the mirror and tell it to yourself. Every retelling strengthens the muscle of truth.

Every time you claim your story, you remind yourself and the world (if you're speaking in public) that using your language is an act of freedom and that voice itself is vibration.

When I think back to all the times I've raced toward a story—through the neon blur of Hollywood or the desert roads of the West Bank—the feeling in my chest was the same. The body doesn't always know the difference between ambition and alarm. It just recognizes frequency. In both places, the air vibrated with truth yearning to be heard. That's what storytelling is at its core. It's a tuning toward what's real beneath the noise, driven by the courage to meet the pitch of the unknown, and stay there long enough to translate it into meaning.

2

LOCAL STORIES AS THE ARCHITECTURE OF INNOVATION AND RESILIENCE

Stories create community, enable us
to see through the eyes of other people,
and open us to the claims of others.

—Peter Forbes, photographer

We ran toward the edge of the hill, breathless, as the canopy behind us caught the wind like a giant pair of lungs. Then the ground disappeared. I was suddenly, gloriously airborne, paragliding over South Africa's wine country—which, for the record, is not a place whose fruits you should thirstily drink from before jumping off a mountain. I felt free and woozy. The land below looked like a living painting of sunlit vineyards, distant purple mountains, and a river curling through orchards like a slip of silver ribbon.

From up there, everything appeared abundant and beautifully arranged. But during the moments of delight and giddiness, I couldn't help but think for a flicker of a moment about how thin the line was between soaring and crashing into the side of the mountain. One rogue gust could pitch us from grace to ruin in seconds. That pretty much sums up how that entire year felt.

It was the end of 2021—that strange, hopeful stretch of the year when corners of the world were starting to open up again after being closed, due to the pandemic. Many of us were relearning how to breathe in public without looking suspicious. Freedom never felt so good—or so sanitized and micromanaged. There were early curfews, one-way grocery aisles, and couples trying to kiss through masks like they were performing a modern-dance routine about desire and longing.

While paragliding, I thought about how boundless and infinite the sky felt. But on the ground, conversations were still tangled in fear, infection rates, conspiracy theories, and loss. It was like the whole planet was workshopping a script no one could agree on. The movie was half disaster, half group therapy session, directed by chaos itself.

COVID-19 was a public health crisis wrapped in a narrative crisis. The world was fractured into competing versions of truth, some grounded in science, others in survival instincts, rumor, or politics. Social distancing separated not only our bodies but our worldviews. Even our stories went into lockdown, staring out the window like they were stuck at daycare, waiting for clarity that never came.

But from up in the air, the villages below weren't divided by fear or politics. They were stitched together by the same landscape and the same human insistence to keep going. From that height, everything made sense—or maybe it was just the wine plus the altitude talking.

Image 2. Paragliding over wine country outside Cape Town. May 2021.

FROM SOUTH AFRICAN SKIES TO TOWNSHIP STREETS

The day after my wine and sky adventure, my feet were planted firmly in Nyanga, one of Cape Town's oldest Black townships,[10] established in the 1940s under apartheid's migrant labor system. While it remains one of the city's economically marginalized areas, it's also known for its entrepreneurial spirit, community networks, and cultural vitality. Here a dance with joy and risk, similar to what I experienced in the sky, played out in very different terms.

[10] "City of Cape Town—2011 Census Suburb Nyanga," Strategic Development Information and GIS Department, July 2013, https://resource.capetown.gov.za/documentcentre/Documents/Maps%20and%20statistics/2011_Census_CT_Suburb_Nyanga_Profile.pdf.

The roads were dusty but electric with life. Children darted barefoot through alleys, while women balanced crates on their heads, and shop doors stood open to catch the breeze. This was resilience and abundance up close, not the well-manicured kind that looks good from the above, but the raw, daily alchemy of turning scarcity into sustenance.

My client, Untapped Global,[11] took my team and me to meet local business owner Khose Lewani at her Pick n Pay shop, where she greeted neighbors by name and laughed with the kind of warmth that made you want to live in her store. Not only did her shop carry essentials, it offered portable canisters of gas from PayGas, a company making clean cooking energy accessible by letting families buy only what they need. This lowered costs and cut carbon emissions. In a community where many households run small businesses from their kitchens, this was a quiet revolution.

"It's amazing," Khosi told me, glancing outside. "Most of these businesses you see like the women selling plates of food and the dressmakers, they're all run by women. They keep this place going."

One young woman, Yolanda, explained that PayGas[12] allowed her to refill gas two or three times a week, spending significantly less than she had previously. Another woman, cooking for her neighbors since 2005, smiled as she said she no longer needed to scrape together the full cost to fill her tank.

I reflected on how perfect the South African land looked from above, a vision of order and prosperity. But it was on the ground in Nyanga's narrow streets that I saw resourcefulness up close. It pulsed through everyday transactions, such as a mother topping up her fuel

---

[11] Untapped Global, accessed September 12, 2025, https://untapped-global.com.

[12] "PayGas Plans to Install 52 Pay-as-You-Gas-Stations in SA," *Clean Cooking Alliance*, July 14, 2020, accessed September 12, 2025. https://cleancooking.org/news/07-14-2020-paygas-plans-to-install-52-pay-as-you-gas-stations-in-sa/.

so she could keep serving plates of steaming stew, or a shopkeeper adjusting her stock to fit the budgets of her neighbors.

I remember thinking, *What if we measured the health of a place not by the size of its export markets or the gleam of its tourist resorts, but by how it nurtures its smallest enterprises? What if instead of calculating GDP, we honored the local resilience of women like Khosi and Yolanda, who transform a few coins into community-led economies?*

When we overlook these hyperlocal stories—when we fail to tell them, invest in them, or learn from them—we miss the heartbeat of how real change takes root. And this was all happening in Nyanga despite systemic neglect, COVID, and every barrier designed to keep progress out.

Image 3. Khosi Liwani, owner of the local Pick n Pay Market Ndwamba in Nyanga, Cape Town, South Africa, being interviewed behind her store. May 2021.

INGENUITY UNDER LOCKDOWN

As I walked through Nyanga's neighborhoods, I thought of Puerto Rico, the island I called home during the pandemic. The human resilience there carries a similar essence. Both places had long histories of being undervalued by larger systems. Both were seen from the outside as fragile, and yet both played on with local ingenuity and resourcefulness.

What I witnessed in South Africa's townships, I was also seeing across Puerto Rican kitchens, workshops, and farms. Everyday people were reimagining survival as innovation, weaving community safety nets when formal institutions fell short.

PHARMA RECLAIMED

During the height of the pandemic, I met Keila López and her co-founders, who built GK Pharmaceuticals, the first pharmaceutical company in the US owned by women of color.[13] In an industry primarily made up of men and dominated by multinational corporations, their venture was an act of reclamation, a voice calling for equity. While they were manufacturing medicine, they were also rewriting the rules of who gets to lead in science and healthcare and anchoring economic power in their own community. For an island

[13] Melissa Jun Rowley, "Meet the Entrepreneur Who Started the First Pharmaceutical Company Owned by Puero Rican Women in the US," *Forbes*, December 31, 2020, https://www.forbes.com/sites/melissarowley/2021/12/31/meet-the-entrepreneur-who-started-the-first-pharmaceutical-company-owned-by-women-of-color-in-the-us/.

long used as a testing ground for pharmaceutical giants, their work was both defiance and declaration.

When most of the world was still frozen in uncertainty, their team led by scientist and chemical engineer Mayra Guzmán-Kaslow, along with her two daughters and childhood best friend, began developing one of the island's first molecular COVID-19 tests.

By July 2020, after months of navigating bureaucracy and pressure, GK Pharmaceuticals became the first and only Puerto Rican company to manufacture an FDA-approved test of its kind. Mayra, a veteran of nearly three decades in regulatory compliance, saw opportunity in returning home. She understood Puerto Rico's legacy as a pharmaceutical hub, an island where twelve of the world's top twenty drug companies once operated, and she wanted to prove that Puerto Ricans could not only manufacture for others, but innovate for themselves. "We are just as capable as men," she told me. "We need more women scientists, chemists, biologists, and engineers."

Their story is a reminder that resilience is rooted in endurance and authorship. In a global crisis defined by fear and scarcity, these women turned knowledge into sovereignty, transforming a system built on extraction into one rooted in local ownership and reinvestment.

SHIELDS FROM A LIVING ROOM

When hospitals across Puerto Rico ran out of protective gear at the height of COVID, María Laura Martínez Kezner and her husband Vicente Gascó Gómez fired up their 3D printer and began producing face shields in their living room.[14] At first, their invention was used exclusively in hospitals as a way to protect the doctors and nurses risking their lives. But soon their makeshift production line became a lifeline across the island.

Friends dropped off supplies, neighbors helped with deliveries, and orders came in faster than they could print. What began as a personal act of service rippled outward, proving how quickly creativity can lead to a solution when urgency demands it.

The couple's design studio, Tredé, teamed up with Luis Torres, founder of Engine-4 Coworking Space, whose fabrication lab housed large-format 3D printers. Together they joined a global maker movement, an informal network of engineers, artists, and citizens who stepped in when supply chains collapsed and government plans failed. The FDA had barely begun to regulate 3D-printed PPE (personal protective equipment) when Puerto Rican makers were already improvising solutions in real time.

Across the island, materials were scarce. Filament, the plastic thread used for printing, had to be imported from the US and Europe, often delayed for weeks. Yet, through donations and community resource-sharing, María and Vicente managed to keep their small operation running. Within weeks, they produced more than 1,500 face shields, collaborating with doctors at El Hospital HIMA San Pablo Cupey to refine each design for comfort and safety.

Tredé's story made news across the world as part of what MAKE Magazine Founder Dale Dougherty called *Plan C*, the maker

[14] Melissa Jun Rowley, "Trailblazers of Puerto Rico: Meet the Couple Making Shields for Healthcare Workers on the Front Lines of COVID-19," *Forbes*, April 11, 2020, https://www.forbes.com/sites/melissarowley/2020/04/10/trailblazers-of-puerto-rico-meet-the-couple-making-shields-for-healthcare-workers-on-the-frontlines-of-covid-19/.

community's "backup plan for the backup plan."[15] When governments faltered and industries stalled, people stepped in to protect one another. In Puerto Rico, that spirit of invention carried an even deeper resonance for an island that's been treated as dependent, proving that its greatest export is its creativity and ingenuity.

FARMING FOR SOVEREIGNTY

Another local Puerto Rican family, Cristian and Cristina González, together with Cristian's father, Luis, stepped forward when global supply chains failed. Through their farm, Finca González, and their direct-to-consumer platform, PRoduce, they connected local harvests to neighborhood households.[16]

Cut off from imports when shipping slowed and store shelves emptied, they harvested greens, packed boxes, and delivered produce straight to neighbors' doors. In a territory where more than 80 percent of food is imported, their work represented far more than convenience; it strengthened food sovereignty. Each box of vegetables proved that Puerto Rico's future did not have to be tethered to ships arriving at the port. It could be grown in its own soil, carried in the arms of its own people, and delivered along roads that larger systems had long overlooked.

---

[15] Dale Dougherty, "Place C: Crisis mode for COVID-19," *Make: Magazine*, March 30, 2020, https://makezine.com/article/maker-news/plan-c-crisis-mode-for-covid-19/.

[16] Melissa Jun Rowley, "How This Family of Founders Is Working to Make Puerto Rico More Self-Sufficient Through Local Farming and Delivery," *Forbes*, April 26, 2020, https://www.forbes.com/sites/melissarowley/2020/04/26/how-this-family-of-founders-is--working-to-make-puerto-rico-more-self-sufficient-through-local-farming--delivery/.

The farmers, makers, and entrepreneurs of Puerto Rico reminded me of the townships of South Africa and that innovation and resilience are built not from abundance, but from necessity.

COLONIAL WEIGHT, CARIBBEAN RHYTHM

It was in Puerto Rico, during the enforced stillness of lockdown, that I got my first taste of how it feels to slow down, to stop chasing thrills and metaphors. I mean, I had no choice. And the truth is my mind, body, and spirit were craving stillness the day I landed on the island months before the pandemic even hit.

I arrived in San Juan running on adrenaline disguised as purpose. But what I really longed for was peace in my heart, calm leading my days, and, more than anything, community.

The Caribbean, with its humid air and flowing tempo, became my teacher. Puerto Rico invited me to listen to the rhythm beneath the noise: the sound of *coquí* frogs after the rain, the waves softening the edges of a long day of work, the people in the streets greeting one another with unspoken understanding. Time worked differently there. Days expanded. Conversations lingered. Most of all, healing arrived for me in a slow unlearning.

I began what I now call my first phase of deprogramming, from the colonial logic that equates worth with speed, visibility, and endless output. I started to see how deeply that logic lived in my nervous systems; how I'd been programmed to believe that to matter, I had to prove myself over and over again: perform, produce, and put my deeper, more human needs last.

The island's cadence insisted on rest, reciprocity, and relational time measured by presence. Stillness became my default mode, and I wasn't alone in that. Around the world, neighbors shared food while never having previously met, musicians played from balconies, and small businesses reinvented themselves overnight. What looked like a pause from the outside was, in truth, regeneration, a reminder that even in isolation interdependence is what keeps us alive.

Puerto Rico gave me this sanctuary, along with local stories of grit and a perspective on decolonization I didn't have access to until I lived there.

Carrying the weight of being colonized twice—first by Spain, then by the United States—some parts of Puerto Rico's history press into the present like magic and others like background music you didn't choose but can't turn off.

You can taste it in the produce that doesn't make it to local shelves because the Jones Act, which requires goods shipped to Puerto Rico to pass through US ports on US vessels,[17] has long stifled the island's economy and prevents many local farmers from selling their food in the very supermarkets that line their towns.

You can hear it in laws written far away for people who never get a vote. Because Puerto Rico, though part of the United States, has no voting representation in Congress and its residents cannot vote in the presidential election.[18] And you can feel it in the whiplash of

---

[17] Russell Hillberry and Manuel I. Jiminez, "The Effect of the Jones Act on Puerto Rico," CATO Institute, *Research Briefs in Economic Policy* No. 380, April 24, 2024, https://www.cato.org/research-briefs-economic-policy/effect-jones-act-puerto-rico.

[18] Tanner Stening, "Can Puerto Ricans Vote in the Presidential Election? What Role Do US Territories Play in Elections?" *Northeastern Global News*, October 28, 2024, https://news.northeastern.edu/2024/10/28/can-puerto-ricans-vote-presidential-election/.

Dánica Coto, "Residents of Puerto Rico Can't Vote for President, but Their Anger at Trump Is Still Shaping the Race," *PBS NewsHour*, October 28, 2024, https://www.pbs.org/newshour/politics/residents-of-puerto-rico-cant-vote-for-president-but-their-anger-at-trump-is-still-shaping-the-race.

being called "family" by Washington while being treated more like the cousin nobody bothers to pick up from the airport.

Living in Puerto Rico, I couldn't escape the contradictions—the fertile land, hardworking farmers, and resourceful entrepreneurs, all navigating a system designed to keep them dependent on the mainland. At the same time, I also couldn't miss the liveliness that reverberated across the island. From San Juan to Rincon, music spilled from doorways onto cobblestone streets. Dancers turned plazas into impromptu stages, and even in the hardest seasons people found ways to celebrate. There was a rhythm to the island that no law could legislate away, a joy that survived even under the weight of an oppressive history.

When you scratch the surface of most places, you see that many of them carry histories marked by colonization, systemic racism, or extractive economies.

But our history does not define us.

What shifts the arc of any place is its people—the intrepid souls who raise their voices, fight for dignity, and create solutions that strengthen the places they call home. They are the heart of transformation, and it's time the spotlight caught up with them.

WHAT THE HEADLINES MISS

Most of the stories that dominate mainstream news are measured by scale, by towering profits, sweeping policies, or soaring GDP. The Western World is conditioned to look for progress in skyscrapers and megaprojects, in billion-dollar acquisitions and dramatic political announcements.

But the first line of any system—economic, ecological, or social—is local. It lives in transactions so small they're almost invisible to the outside eye. Think of a South African woman refilling her fuel canister with just enough gas to keep her restaurant open another day or a shopkeeper like Khosi deciding to stock cleaner energy because she knows exactly who it will help and how it will support the health of her community.

These stories reveal where and how resilience is truly built in the ingenuity of people who refuse to let scarcity dictate how they live their lives.

When I work with organizations or movements trying to shift systems, I always return to the question: *Whose stories are we telling?*

The stories we tell and consume show us what to value, what to replicate, and what to scale. And when we consistently overlook the hyperlocal—when we fail to elevate voices like Khosi's, Yolanda's, Keila's, and Mayra's—we reinforce an illusion that meaningful change only happens from the top down.

In truth, the future is being drafted daily in places like Nyanga, Cape Town, South Africa, and San Juan, Puerto Rico. It's being cultivated in every choice to spend a few coins on cleaner fuel, in every woman who cooks meals so her neighbors can eat. When these decisions are multiplied across thousands of communities, they set entirely new courses for climate resilience, economic dignity, and public health. When we change whose stories we center, we change what the world invests in, legislates for, and dreams possible.

YOUR MIC CHECK

You constantly move through places where the human experience unfolds. This happens on sidewalks, in kitchens, in small exchanges that never make headlines. You witness the ways people adapt, improvise, care for one another, and keep going when systems fail them. You carry fragments of those moments with you, whether you realize it or not.

Think about the places you know intimately like the corner store where the owner remembers your name, the car shop that stays open late for people, the neighbor who snowplows everyone's driveway without anyone having to ask. These are more than background details. They're hyperlocal stories that make communities work.

Rather than asking what story you *should* tell, this is a chance to explore what you already know about your surroundings and your place in them.

- What patterns have you witnessed over time?
- What kinds of labor, support or improvisation do you see people repeating?
- What moments linger with you long after they're over because they revealed something deeply human and relatable or remarkable?

Often, the most revealing stories of how a city, town, or neighborhood functions aren't the loud ones being recorded or livestreamed. They're the moments showing how people adjust, adapt, and keep going when no one is watching.

TURN UP THE VOLUME

Once you've tuned your ear, here are some ways to amplify local stories and see your role inside of them.

Start at street level. Look at the smallest transactions, like the local fruit vendor bringing food to the homeless or the barber shop giving discounts to people who just lost their jobs. These "micro" stories are the building blocks of macro change.

1. **Name the Trade-offs.** There's no need to sand down the rough edges. Resilience is rarely clean. By showing compromise and imperfection, you make solutions more believable and funders more accountable.
2. **Frame Agency, Not Pity.** Too many global narratives position low-income communities as waiting to be rescued. We can flip that script. Show how people are already solving, innovating, and refusing to become a statistic.
3. **Follow Sideways Growth.** Pay attention to models that spread laterally, like a microfranchise adapted from one township to another or a recycling program replicated across villages. These are the stories of scale that policymakers miss.
4. **Center Local Storytellers.** If the spirit moves you, collaborate with local reporters, artists, and organizers. A story that strengthens visibility and investment on the ground is a story that leaves a legacy.

THE DROP

When I think back to paragliding over South Africa's vineyards, I remember how free I felt and how quickly one rogue gust could have turned my flight into a disaster. It's easy to mistake that kind of adrenaline-fed weightlessness for the heart of a story.

But I found the heart grounded in the dusty streets of Nyanga, where women were determined to keep their kitchens warm and their families fed. Thousands of miles away, this same determination showed up in Keila López reclaiming a pharmaceutical industry that once shut her out and in María's and Vincent's living-room-turned-production-hub for survival.

Resilience doesn't announce itself on a stage or in a press release. It grows in classrooms, corner shops, farms, book clubs, and in all the other everyday ways of life that endure. And if we learn to tell those stories fully and fiercely, they not only diversify the larger narrative of a place or group of people, they change who gets to author the future.

3

THE STORIES WE INHERIT AND THE TRUTH WE CREATE

When we change the story we tell ourselves,
we change the future we create.

—Brené Brown, researcher and author

I was twelve years old, pushing two girls I babysat on the swings at the same playground I'd raced across a hundred times as a child. We were in a small, scrappy park in my Michigan hometown, ringed by trees and a chain-link fence. It was a familiar and safe spot in the way childhood places are—until they're not.

Suddenly, a boy I didn't recognize wandered over, picked up a rock, and hurled it toward me.

"Gook!" he shouted. "Go back to where you came from!"

The rock missed my head and instead nicked my shoulder. But the words he used hit hard.

I had only ever heard "gook" once before, at a young age, viewing a Vietnam War movie that I probably shouldn't have been watching. I didn't fully understand the history of that term, but I understood that it carried bad things like rage, disgust, and the clear message that I didn't belong.

That moment split something open in me as a person. I didn't have the words for it then, standing there with my hands on the swing chains, as heat crawled up my neck. I only knew that part of the way I saw myself was now tangled up with the way a stranger chose to see me.

That's the thing about identity. It's easy to let others define it for us, especially when we're still learning how to stand firmly in who we are and when we're still discerning our stories.

Not all the stories we hold onto were chosen by us. Some were handed to us or even forcibly thrown at us during childhood, projected from the pain, assumptions, and aspirations of others.

Some internal stories we write ourselves in moments of struggle while trying to find a direct path through a maze of misunderstanding, missed opportunities, or hormones. A few were whispered to us by our culture, by classrooms, and by the biases of those around us.

And then there are the stories we repeat silently and subconsciously, the ones that creep up on us and start to sound like the truth. Those less than, not good enough, not cool enough, not impressive enough, not doing enough stories that simply aren't true. But perhaps we don't question them enough. I know I don't.

Owning our birthrights as storytellers begins with asking questions.

Here are some to ponder:

> What if the story that says "Your value depends on your productivity" wasn't your story to begin with?

What if the story that says "You always have to smile, stay agreeable, or keep the peace" is bogus and was never meant for you?

What if the story that says "You're hard to be with or love" was planted by someone who didn't have the capacity to love themselves, let alone another person?

Not only do the negative stories we tell ourselves influence how we see the world, they dictate what we believe we're allowed to ask from it. And while we can't go back and rewrite our past, we can absolutely reframe the way we carry it.

Sometimes a single sentence spoken once in passing can take up permanent residence in our minds. A teacher or boss who said you weren't a strong writer or communicator can cause insecurity for years to come.

A parent who made your sensitivity feel like a liability can lead you to believe you're weak.

Some random person you meet in passing who called you "too ambitious" or said you "keep to yourself too much" with a smile (that wasn't meant to be kind) can piss you off for days.

These moments can end up becoming internal headlines. And when that happens we stop questioning whether or not they're valid, and we slide into living by them.

That's why we need to remember that every great story has subtext and nuance. Perhaps what we thought was a moment of failure was actually a story about growth. As cliche as it sounds, sometimes what looked like rejection was redirection, or at the minimum, an opportunity to look at a situation from a different perspective. Maybe in that moment when you felt broken and like you were losing everything, you were also cultivating your discernment.

And maybe that's the greatest story you'll ever tell—your own story of transformation.

Rewriting your personal narrative doesn't require you to forget about what's happened in your life. It begins with deciding what your most memorable moments mean to you now.

THE STORY I WAS GIVEN

Sometimes the stories we're handed at birth are merely placeholders, myths stitched together with white lies, possibly meant to protect us (or others) or to make us feel special.

I've always known I was adopted. It wasn't something that had to be unveiled in a dramatic moment. It was a knowing that lived in the background of my childhood—steady and familiar like the changing seasons in Michigan.

My parents never kept it from me. They talked about it with openness and grace, encouraging me to ask questions about where I was from, Seoul, Korea. I wasn't their biological child, but I was theirs. That was my first story, and within that story, I was chosen.

For most of my childhood, I wore the badge of being chosen with honor. At school, when my teacher asked us to draw our family trees, I added a note at the bottom that read, *Adopted from South Korea at five months old.*[19] It made me feel distinct, not necessarily different.

---

[19] "History of Adoption in Korea," Korean Adoption Services, accessed November 15, 2025, https://www.kadoption.or.kr/en/info/info_history.jsp.

According to this source, approximately 150,000 children from South Korea have been adopted internationally since the Korean War: Kim Tong-Hyung and Claire Galofaro, "Adoption Fraud Separated Generations of South Korean Children from Their Families, AP Finds," *PBS Frontline*, September 14, 2024, https://www.pbs.org/wgbh/frontline/article/korean-children-adoption-fraud/.

It felt more like I had an interesting backstory instead of a missing identity, even though I had a high school teacher who insisted that I must have struggled with knowing who I was. How could I not, she asked? I didn't. What I struggled with was people projecting their own misunderstandings of international adoption onto me.

My parents reinforced the narrative that I was distinct but not different. So did the photo albums, the baby books, and all the adoption records written in Korean that my mom thoughtfully had laminated, so that we could preserve some small part of my origin.

But stories often change depending on who's listening, who's asking, and what part of you, the storyteller, is ready to be seen. The first time I noticed a crack in my adoption story, I was sitting at a childhood friend's dinner table, eating spaghetti off a Melmac plate. Her younger siblings were peppering me with questions, the unfiltered kind kids often ask.

Did I sit at the dinner table with my family during meals? Did I sleep in a bedroom or the garage?

I responded to these inquiries easily. At the time, I thought they were just curious. Later, I began to realize what I was actually doing for a few members of their family. I was smoothing out the edges of their discomfort, making adoption sound simple, so they wouldn't have to feel awkward.

Those early questions didn't bother me, not yet. But they initiated a slow awareness that the story I had been told at home, the one built on love and gratitude and being "chosen," wasn't the story everyone else saw.

Years later, adolescence took hold. The shift came fast and sharp. Isn't that how it always is when kids become pre-teens and then teens? It feels like the change happens overnight, like a light switch flipped in the dark. But in truth, the evolution had been unfolding in plain sight all along, visible to anyone paying attention.

My questions got louder. So did my silences. The story I'd once recited so confidently started to feel less special and original and more like I was reading from a script someone else had written. The fairytale of being chosen turned darker, more complicated.

I began to wonder why I'd been left on the steps of a police station in Seoul, Korea, the day I was born, another story I was told at a young age. What if I had simply been rehomed like an afterthought, a case file shuffled from one place to another, a decision made for someone else's convenience?

I started asking questions I hadn't given much thought to when I was a kid. Who was my birth mother, really? Why didn't she want me?

WHEN THE STORY GETS TWISTED

During middle school, a part of me shrank. I became increasingly aware that I looked different than all the white kids the student body predominantly consisted of. There was a handful of seventh graders that reminded me of this every day. I'd always known I was Asian and noticed most of the people around me in my small Midwestern town were Caucasian. But now I cared. Suddenly, I saw myself as "other."

As I got older, the story that I had been left on the police station steps the day I was born began to feel less like history and more like a blank space disguised as fact. I wondered how many details had been scrubbed, how many truths had been made palatable for the sake of paperwork or for someone else's peace.

WHEN THE SILENCE BREAKS

Two decades later, I found myself at a conference in Seoul. I didn't go to Korea looking for my birth family, at least not consciously. But I did go with a plan to visit my adoption agency. I went there between sessions, not expecting more than maybe a polite smile, a scan of my records, or another version of the story I had already been told.

The woman who met with me was warm and unabashedly open. She told me she was an adoptee, too, and this work was personal to her. And then, just as casually, as if she were commenting on the weather, she said, "Now let's talk about your birth search."

"Oh, I'm not here to do a birth search. I just wanted to learn about the state of adoption in Korea today. Besides, I was told there are no records of my birth mother anywhere."

"That's not true."

I sat up straighter. "What do you mean?"

"Your birth mother didn't leave you at a police station," she said. "She brought you to a missionary on Jeju Island, and the missionary brought you to an orphanage. Your mother left her name and her address."

Suddenly, the floor beneath me shifted. Years of imagining abandonment gave way to something more complex and infinitely more human. My birth mother had not disappeared into the shadows. She had done what she could.

"Can I see the information?" I asked, already knowing the answer.

She shook her head. "I'm sorry. It's against Korean adoption law. I can't share it."

For a moment, I felt everything at once. Anger. Relief. Sorrow for the years I had spent believing a story that wasn't mine. Gratitude that someone, somewhere, had tried to do the right thing. I thought about lunging across the desk, grabbing the file, and running. But I didn't. Instead, I kept listening.

"I have other information that might be of interest to you," she said. "Would you like to see a photo of your Korean foster mother, the woman who took care of you here in Seoul before you were sent to America?"

I nodded. She handed over a pile of documents along with an old identification card of a woman I never had the chance to know or thank for taking care of me.

"All of our foster mothers love the babies they watch over so much," she added.

Suddenly, I had a new birth story, one featuring three mothers who made my life possible—my birth mother, my foster mother, and my mom.

What I learned replaced the narrative I'd been told since childhood. The story of abandonment had never been mine. It had simply been the one that was available.

While this new truth didn't fill in all the gaps, it gave weight to the part of me that had always wondered, *What if that wasn't the whole story?*

I didn't feel transformed. But I felt something inside me start to settle, the way your body does when it finally receives a shot of air or drink of water after holding your breath for too long.

And that was enough.

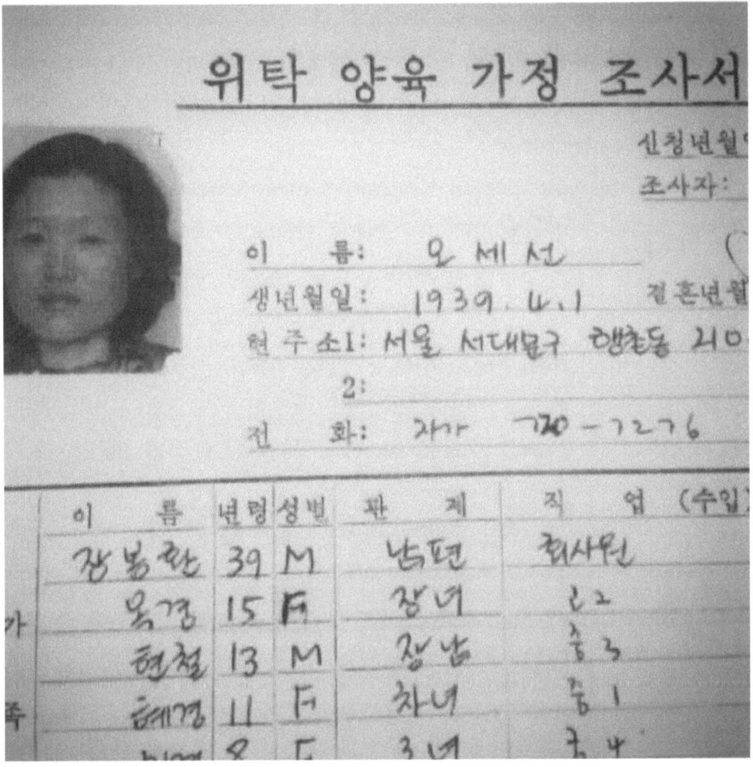

위탁 양육 가정 조사서

신청년월일
조사자:

이 름: 오세선
생년월일: 1939. 4. 1　결혼년월
현 주소1: 서울 서대문구 행촌동 210
2:
전 화: 자가 7[illegible]0-7276

가족	이 름	년령	성별	관 계	직 업 (수입)
	장봉환	39	M	남편	회사원
	옥경	15	F	장녀	고2
	현철	13	M	장남	중3
	혜경	11	F	차녀	중1
	[illegible]	8	F	3녀	[illegible]

Image 4. A picture of my foster mother's file retrieved through the Holt International Adoption Agency in Seoul, Korea.

THE GREAT REWRITE

Isn't it funny? The past is just a story we tell ourselves.

—From the movie *Her* (2013)

The stories we're given about who we are, what we're worth, and where we came from are often passed on to us like hand-me-downs.

Sometimes they're well-intentioned. Sometimes they're distorted. Often, they're incomplete. And at some point, we may start to realize that certain stories don't quite fit anymore. That realization is where the new story begins.

Rewriting your personal narrative means reclaiming your role as the author and narrator, not just a character being acted upon. When we rewrite a story about our own worth, we disrupt systems that thrive on us doubting it. When we challenge the narratives we inherited about race, gender, or identity, we create space for others to do the same. When we tell the truth about who we are and what we've survived, we expose gaps in the systems that were supposed to protect us.

Like anything worth changing within, the shift doesn't happen in a single moment. It unfolds in practice, in noticing the story you keep telling yourself on repeat, and deciding that you want to tell it differently.

YOUR MIC CHECK

Think about the stories that you believe have shaped your personality and attitude the most, not the ones you proudly claim in your bio, but the ones projected onto you before you were old enough to know better. Maybe there was a teacher who told you you weren't smart enough or a coach who said you weren't tough enough or a family member or romantic partner who praised you for being "easy" or punished you for being "complicated." These instances were part of a culture that taught you that in order to belong you had to be a certain way.

Notice what happens in your body when you recall one of these stories. Does your chest tighten? Do your shoulders rise? Do you stop breathing when those memories surface? That somatic reaction is your mic check.

Repeating a story for years doesn't make it true. It just makes it familiar. And familiarity is not the same as truth.

TURN UP THE VOLUME

Rewriting our narrative starts with reclaiming ourselves.

- **Name the Story:** Write down one story you've told yourself again and again about your worth, your capability, or your sense of belonging.
- **Excavate the Source:** Ask where it came from. A parent, a friend or frenemy, a script someone projected? Naming the origin shifts the weight because that's when we start to see that a story was inherited, not inevitable.
- **Reframe with Compassion:** Imagine this story belonged to someone you love. How would you narrate it differently? Offer yourself the same kindness and generosity.
- **Rewrite the Lines:** Flip one phrase that has haunted you. "Too sensitive" becomes "I notice what others miss." "Too ambitious" becomes "I am expansive." Give yourself permission to speak it aloud until it begins to feel like it was always yours.

This practice can help build muscle for creating a new narrative. It doesn't happen once. It unfolds daily, in conversations, in moments of solitude, and in doing random things like taking a shower, working out at the gym, walking your dog, grocery shopping, or driving your kids to school.

Just as the stories imposed on you by fear, survival, or by other people's pain or expectations took root through repetition, a new story can take hold the same way. The stories we live inside are learned. That means they can also be rewritten.

THE DROP

Every time you choose a kinder narrative, you make it harder for the older one to win. And every time you reclaim your story, you remind others that they can do the same. The people watching you begin to see new possibilities for themselves. That is the miracle of storytelling.

You are not only the main character of your story. You are the author and the narrator. You hold the pen. And the moment you decide to think and write differently about who you are, you alter the map for everyone who follows.

PART 2

FINDING THE POCKET

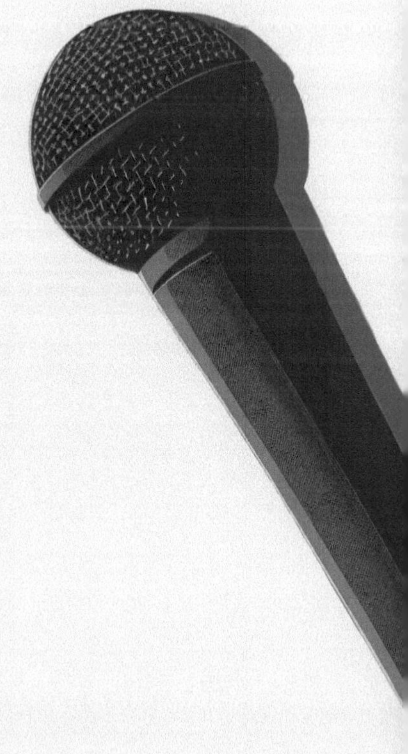

4

POLICY IS PERSONAL: WHERE LAW MEETS DAILY LIFE

Stories change policy because they change what we can see. When people can see one another's realities, solutions become possible.

—Ai-jen Poo, in multiple interviews about narrative power and domestic worker legislation

I was ten years old when I raised my right hand and swore the oath to become an American citizen. The words were lofty and heady, too formal for a child. But I knew they were important. They were becoming a part of my identity. From that day forward, my future was tethered to a piece of paper. It was legal proof that I belonged in a country that is ironically still struggling to decide who counts and who doesn't.

In 2025, that memory beckons me to time travel as I watch immigration raids unfold across the US. Families are being separated.[20] Workers are being deported. Children are being ripped from their parents and left behind. These tragedies trace directly back to policy—to laws written years ago, decisions about how they're enforced today, and the absence of protections where they should exist but don't.

In our lifetimes, policy has determined whose safety is prioritized, whose labor is exploited, and whose absence is part of the status quo.

Earlier this year, a federal appeals court upheld policy changes that ended Temporary Protected Status (TPS) and restricted humanitarian parole programs that had offered refuge to hundreds of thousands of people from Cuba, Haiti, Nicaragua, and Venezuela. These include families who have worked, studied, and raised children in the US for years.[21] Decisions that blur the lines between TPS and parole protections are now being challenged in federal courts, leaving many immigrants in a state of legal limbo and fear of forced return.

In California, recent Immigration and Customs Enforcement (ICE) operations have disrupted the farm-labor workforce, leaving fields partially harvested and crops spoiling in the sun. According to one recent study modeling the 2025 raids in key agricultural districts,[22] these actions have sharply reduced available labor and

---

[20] Andrew Chung, "US Supreme Court Backs Trump on Aggressive Immigration Raids," *Reuters*, September 8, 2025, https://www.reuters.com/world/us/us-supreme-court-backs-trump-aggressive-immigration-raids-2025-09-08.

[21] Michael Casey, "Appeals Court Rules Trump Administration Can End Legal Protections for More than 400,000 Migrants," *The Associated Press*, September 12, 2025, https://apnews.com/article/ef3eb9ff1a2728fadc2f76f865086b2c.

[22] Xinyu Li, "Quantifying the Economic Impact of 2025 ICE Raids on California's Agricultural Industry: A Case Study of Oxnard," Cornell University, submitted August 5, 2025, https://doi.org/10.48550/arXiv.2508.03787.

destabilized local economies, impacting supply chains and likely contributing to higher food costs. Strawberries rot on the vine while families who once picked them vanish from the community, leaving behind both economic loss and an aching silence in the rows.[23]

And behind the raids, deportations, and status-terminations lies a deeper crisis of disregard for due process, the legal protections that ensure a hearing, representation, and a chance to be seen. In 2025, courts flagged how policies that speed removal and halt appeals may violate the Fifth Amendment rights of immigrants and residents alike.

Immigration law may be drafted in the language of enforcement, but it is lived in the language of absence, such as an empty chair at the table, a missing worker in the field, or a child waiting for a parent who may never return.

These stories make visible how policy moves through ordinary lives. In the same vein, stories can move policy.

WHEN TESTIMONY BECOMES POLICY

At the University of California, Davis, the project Humanizing Deportation has created one of the largest open-access archives of migrant testimonies in the world.[24] Participants collaborate to create digital stories in their own voice.

---

[23] Tim Reid, et al., "Immigration Raids Leave Crops Unharvested, California Farms at Risk," *Reuters*, updated June 30, 2025, https://www.reuters.com/business/immigration-raids-leave-crops-unharvested-california-farms-risk-2025-06-30/.

[24] "About the Project," Humanizing Deportation, University of California, Davis, accessed November 15, 2025, https://humanizandoladeportacion.ucdavis.edu/en/about-the-project/.

Across the archives, people describe early-morning raids, abrupt removals from their homes, and the disorienting journeys that follow. Some recount being taken without warning, given little time to gather belongings, and being transported across long distances in silence. Others speak about the aftermath including missed years with children and the slow work of rebuilding life from the margins. These testimonies insist on something policy language often avoids: deportation is not simply a procedure. It is a rupture in a human life.

When I first scrolled through the Humanizing Deportation archive, I had to stop after just a few videos. The rawness was overwhelming. There was no external narration or editorial framing, just people speaking directly about what it means to be rendered disposable by a system. It was impossible not to feel implicated as a citizen, as a writer, and as someone whose belonging is secured by paperwork that others are denied.

That same insistence on first-person truth is driving broader efforts to shift immigration policy. The nonprofit Freedom for Immigrants[25] has built a narrative-change campaign led by people who have survived immigration detention. The effort goes beyond documenting abuse inside detention centers, aiming instead to dismantle the detention system itself. Former detainees speak in congressional briefings, lead community teach-ins, and shape media campaigns in which their voices are not reduced to soundbites.

Across the campaign, survivors describe the lingering effects of detention long after release, including the constant surveillance,

[25] "Narrative Change," Freedom for Immigrants, accessed November 15, 2025, https://www.freedomforimmigrants.org/narrative-change.

the sleep disruption, the bodily stress that follows them into freedom. When these accounts are shared before lawmakers and the public, detention is no longer framed as administrative or procedural. It is revealed as a form of state-sanctioned trauma.

Listening to Freedom for Immigrants' work, I was struck by how rare it remains for lawmakers to hear directly from those most impacted by immigration policy. Too often, stories are filtered through nonprofits, reporters, or statistics. In this campaign, survivors refuse that mediation. They take the mic and reset the frame.

Across these projects runs a common truth. Policy shifts when those most affected tell their own stories and insist on being heard, and when citizens listen, respond, and act in solidarity.

WHEN FEAR REDRAWS THE GUEST LIST

Like many people across the United States, I feel the reverberations of fear in my own community. Friends are cancelling travel plans because they don't trust they'll be let back in. Colleagues are apprehensive about bringing family members to events in case an expired document puts them at risk. Even at conferences in rooms bursting with privilege, I hear the edge in people's voices, the light concern about whether or not they'll be questioned at customs, or worse, detained just for showing up.

Absence tells a story. At the 2025 United Nations General Assembly and Climate Week NYC, the rooms were different in that they weren't as colorful or diverse as previous years. Fewer Indigenous leaders made the trip. Fewer participants from the Global South were able to attend. Even several colleagues of mine from Europe stayed home. Their concerns revolved around visas, paperwork, and the border itself. They faced the question of whether or not being detained, interrogated, or barred from entry was a risk worth taking. And who could blame them? They had every reason to take pause.

When the people most impacted by climate collapse and systemic injustice can't get to the tables where decisions are made, the narrative is worse than incomplete. It's unjust. A narrowed narrative means narrowed solutions.

This, too, makes me think back to the ten-year-old me, raising her hand to take the oath of citizenship, trusting that a piece of paper meant belonging. Decades later, I see how fragile that promise remains. On paper, the US promises due process to anyone on its soil—citizen or not.

The Fifth Amendment says no person shall be deprived of liberty without that protection. But in practice, the right depends on where you're caught, what documents you have in your pocket, and whether or not you can afford a lawyer.

Through policies like expedited removal, people can be deported within days, often without ever seeing a judge.[26] Four out of five detained immigrants face court alone. The backlog now stretches into the millions. The law says due process exists, but in reality, it's rationed.

Immigration isn't the only place where that gap appears. Across every system, narrative precedes policy. The stories that dominate public imagination determine which reforms rise and which never reach the page.

* * *

---

[26] "Fact Sheet: Expanded Expedited Removal," *National Immigration Forum*, May 14, 2025, https://forumtogether.org/article/fact-sheet-expanded-expedited-removal/.

WHEN STORIES CHANGE WORKPLACE POLICY

I first learned about Suzette Wright's story during the #MeToo movement, reading a New York Times exposé on sexual harassment at Ford.[27] While her story was told through the lens of her individual workplace experience, it gave readers a look into an entire system of power that demanded silence from women who needed that system's paychecks to survive.

Suzette was a single mother who had landed what should have been a breakthrough job at Ford's Chicago Assembly Plant in the 1990s. The paycheck tripled what she had made as a receptionist. It promised stability for her and her child. But what came with it was relentless harassment in the form of crude comments, groping, and intimidation. This was so ingrained in the work culture that speaking up meant risking everything. So for years she kept her head down.

Then #MeToo changed the rules. When Suzette finally told her story, she helped force Ford to overhaul harassment training and put safeguards in place for women on the line.

I was so moved by Suzette's courage and story that I invited her to participate in the *Time for Solutions Summit*, organized by Futures Without Violence,[28] an organization that for nearly forty years has

---

[27] Susan Chira and Catrin Einhorn, "How tough is it to change a culture of harassment? Ask the women of Ford," *New York Times*, December 19, 2017, https://www.nytimes.com/interactive/2017/12/19/us/ford-chicago-sexual-harassment.html.

[28] Sarah Gonzalez Bocinski, "Time for Solutions," *Futures Without Violence blog*, May 15, 2018, https://futureswithoutviolence.org/news/time-for-solutions-summit/.

worked to help families and communities thrive, free from violence through advocacy, prevention programs, and policy change.

When Suzette stood on stage in front of lawmakers, activists, and corporate leaders, I saw firsthand how her new narrative shifted their posture. She turned her pain into testimony, demonstrating how storytelling can shift the ground beneath policy.

TURNING PERSONAL SURVIVAL INTO LAW

Throughout my travels, so many women I've met along the way have provided an oasis of hope in every storm of doubt. Karla Hernández is notably one of them. I met Karla when I was writing about gender-based violence in Puerto Rico.[29] She had been raped in December 2020, and was forced to navigate a justice system that compounded her trauma at every turn. Evidence sat untouched for years. Bureaucratic delays stretched endlessly. Some officials treated her case like an inconvenience.

When Karla shared her experience with me, I was shocked by the neglect and slammed doors she encountered. But once her story was published for the world to see, something powerful happened. Women began reaching out to her in droves. They recognized themselves in her words, they trusted her with their

[29] Melissa Jun Rowley, "Women of Puerto Rico Unite to Bring Justice to Victims of Domestic Violence & Sexual Assault," *Forbes*, May 12, 2021, https://www.forbes.com/sites/melissarowley/2021/05/12/women-of-puerto-rico-unite-to-bring-justice-to-victims-of-domestic-violence--sexual-assault/.

Melissa Jun Rowley, "Building a Culture of Courage and Accountability this Sexual Assault Awareness Month and Beyond," *Rolling Stone*, Culture Council, April 15, 2025, https://www.rollingstone.com/culture-council/articles/building-courage-accountability-sexual-assault-awareness-beyond-1235317002/.

own traumas. Suddenly, in addition to being a survivor, Karla was a point of connection in a much larger chorus of voices demanding change.

Those voices inspired Karla and her husband, Gerald Ericksen, to draft Puerto Rico's first Victims' Bill of Rights. The proposed legislation is designed to guarantee timely processing of evidence, access to services, and enforceable protections for survivors. Out of this effort, Karla created Vivo Alliance,[30] a nonprofit built to channel survivor voices into advocacy and accountability.

By 2024, Vivo Alliance had partnered with the Joyful Heart Foundation[31] to investigate Puerto Rico's rape kit backlog and expose systemic failures. The bill is still making its way through legislative processes, but the shift has already begun. Karla's story, woven with the broader context of systemic injustice, opened the door for others to step forward and grab the mic.

TURNING PAIN INTO PROTECTION

Stories like Karla's remind us that pain can be alchemized into purpose, and hopefully, ultimately policy. This idea transcends geography and circumstances.

I was reminded of this when I met Kevin and Maggie Hines in New York during the United Nations General Assembly. Kevin is one of only a few people in history to survive a jump from the Golden Gate Bridge. At nineteen, in the grip of a mental

---

[30] Vivo Alliance, https://www.vivoalliance.org.

[31] Joyful Heart Foundation, https://www.joyfulheartfoundation.org/about-us/our-mission/.

health crisis, he leapt only to realize midair that he wanted to live. Against all odds, he survived. And his story is now the cornerstone of speeches he gives about what it means to wrestle with despair and choose life.

When Kevin tells his story, he doesn't stop at the shift he felt inside after he jumped. He connects it to policy. For decades, families and advocates pleaded for suicide deterrent nets to be installed along the Golden Gate Bridge. The idea was dismissed and delayed.

Kevin kept testifying. He kept telling lawmakers and the public that stories can save lives and so can safeguards. His voice joined thousands of others, until the pressure became undeniable.

In January 2024, the Golden Gate Bridge completed the installation of a continuous physical suicide-deterrent system spanning the full 1.7 miles of the bridge, a stainless-steel net suspended twenty feet below the deck, designed to save lives and honor decades of advocacy by survivors and families.[32]

When Kevin handed me a copy of his book *Cracked, Not Broken* after we met, I dove into it as soon as I got home.[33] Page after page, I saw how a single human story told with unflinching honesty can bend hearts and minds. Kevin's testimony positioned suicide prevention as a public responsibility that called for policy.

---

[32] "Suicide Deterrent Net: Saving Lives at the Golden Gate Bridge," Golden Gate Bridge, Highway and Transportation District, accessed October 20, 2025, https://www.goldengate.org/district/district-projects/suicide-deterrent-net/.

[33] Kevin Hines, *Cracked, Not Broken: Surviving and Thriving After a Suicide Attempt* (Rowman & Littlefield Publishers, 2013).

YOUR MIC CHECK

If you're fighting to change a law, challenge a system, or introduce a policy, here are some storytelling strategies to support you.

1. **Make It Personal, not Abstract.** Policymakers are inundated with data, statistics, and reports. But that's not what moves them. What moves anyone is emotion.
   - Factual: "There are 100,000 untested rape kits in the US"
   - Personal: "My rape kit sat on a shelf for five years while my rapist walked free."

   Numbers are easy to ignore, but a survivor's voice is palpable.
2. **Find the Unexpected Messenger.** Sometimes the most effective voices for a cause aren't the ones you'd expect. Climate policy debates broadened when veterans framed climate change as a national security threat. Anti-smoking campaigns accelerated when physicians began publicly linking cigarettes to lung cancer and heart disease.

   Ask yourself who in your movement can break through political silos?
3. **Offer a Clear Solution.** A good story makes people care. A great story gives them something to do about it.

   Tip: End every advocacy pitch with a clear policy ask. This could be a specific law, funding allocation, or reform that needs to happen.
4. **Speak to the Heart and the Head.** Legislators may vote with their logic, but they listen with their emotions.
   - Lead with a personal story to create connection. Back it up with data to reinforce credibility.
   - And end with a *call to action* to drive change.

WRITE THE STORY YOU WANT THE WORLD TO BELIEVE

Laws change when enough people demand a different future. Your story could be a catalyst.

It's not enough to reframe old narratives. Reframing can shift language, but it rarely changes the deeper structures. To create lasting change, we need new narratives that challenge the status quo while offering something better, more equitable, and more humane.

That's what Suzette Wright did when she broke the silence about harassment at Ford. Her words exposed abuse and pushed a multibillion-dollar company to reckon with its culture. It's what Karla Hernández and Gerald Ericksen did in Puerto Rico when they drafted a Victims' Bill of Rights turning pain into a framework for justice. And it's what Kevin Hines did by carrying his story from the Golden Gate Bridge into rooms where policy was debated until deterrent nets were finally approved.

Each of these examples show that while storytelling often recounts trauma, it also builds blocks for new narratives that cause lawmakers, corporations, and communities to stretch beyond old, stagnant, or harmful norms.

TURN UP THE VOLUME

Turning testimony into policy requires clarity and strategy.

When Suzette spoke at the Futures Without Violence *Time for Solutions Summit*, I watched a roomful of business leaders and advocates lean forward in their chairs. Her story ignited a collective urge in them to change the workplace and make women safe on the line.

Story plus strategy equals leverage.

Here are some ways to spark that kind of movement.

- **Make Your Story Lived.** The image of a child detained by ICE will outlast data. So will a teenager filming officers handcuff his father on their front porch, or a 6 a.m. knock at the door that turns a quiet kitchen into a scene of zip-tied wrists.
- **Name the Structure at Fault.** Stories that change policy are rarely about a single person's pain. They include a tremendous backlog of examples of struggle and corruption. Always connect the dots.
- **Pair the Story with an Ask.** A father describing his arrest on a front porch also calls for limits on warrantless home raids. A student who watched her mother taken at a traffic stop demands access to legal counsel. Empathy without an ask evaporates.
- **Protect the Storyteller.** Storytelling is powerful, but it is also vulnerable. Survivors, immigrants, and workers should be centered, supported, and shielded from exploitation.
- **Build the Chorus.** One voice can open the door. A hundred voices can keep it from closing.

THE DROP

Every corrupt or dangerous system looks unshakable until someone names the truth out loud. Then the cracks appear.

Policy can impact who gets to work, who makes it home for dinner, and even who feels safe enough to tell their story.

Every law and reform begins as someone's story carried into the light and amplified with strategy. When you tell your story with clarity and courage, you aren't only speaking for yourself. You're expanding the realms of what policy can be. You're shifting who gets heard and who gets protected.

Policy may be written on paper, but it is powered by voices. And as long as voices keep rising, the shape of the law is never finished.

5

POLICY IS COLLECTIVE: WHEN MOVEMENTS FIND THEIR VOICE

Changing policy requires changing the narrative. We can't repair systems until we change the stories that built them.

—Bryan Stevenson, executive director, Equal Justice Initiative, Montgomery, Alabama

It was a hot, stifling afternoon in the desert, filled with the kind of heat that clings to your skin even indoors. While roaming Dubai's Expo City, the host of COP28, the UN's annual global climate convening, I found myself wandering through a maze of exhibition halls. To say I was feeling dehydrated and frustrated by how massively spread out and confusing I found the conference grounds would be an understatement. Finally, I gave up searching for my next session, bought an ice cream cone, and collapsed onto a bench. As the cold sweetness cut through the haze, I felt human again.

That's when I took in the scene around me and noticed the diversity of the crowd. Indigenous elders in woven sashes walked slowly past carbon market traders in crisp suits. Philanthropists rushed by youth activists with handmade signs. Grassroots organizers clustered near water coolers networking with UN directors. Climate tech bros pitched their startups to venture capitalists, while checking their phones between meetings. Expo City felt like a conference Babel, with each group speaking its own language of climate action against a backdrop of geopolitical agendas.

While strawberry and peanut butter swirl dripped down my face, another thought surfaced. No matter the vocabulary or strategy, most people there ultimately wanted the same thing—to protect our people and our planet. But we hadn't formed a united front.

That's when it hit me: What if, instead of staying in our corners, we rallied behind one story? By the end of the week, it happened. A campaign called *Later is Too Late*, which initially began as a climate sentiment that surfaced in research and discourse coming out of Yale University, brought 800 leaders together to push for language committing governments to "transition away from fossil fuels"—for the first time ever.[34]

---

[34] "Shaping Tomorrow: Time for Better's Impact on COP 28's 'Later Is Too Late' Campaign," Time for Better, accessed October 2025, https://timeforbetter.org/agency-news/shaping-tomorrow-timeforbetters-impact-cop28s-lateristoolate-campaign.

"Later Is Too Late: Impact Report," Time for Better, February 7, 2024, https://timeforbetter.org/wp-content/uploads/2024/02/TimeforBetter-LaterisTooLate-ImpactReport24-004o-NOLOGO.pdf.

"COP28 Ends with Call to Transition Away from Fossil Fuels," *United Nations News*, December 13, 2023, https://news.un.org/en/story/2023/12/1144742.

Organizations including The B Team, EarthRise Studio, Global Optimism, and Time for Better led the charge. My phone buzzed nonstop for days as colleagues, friends, and strangers reposted the same message, *later is too late.*

I joined thousands of others in amplifying it, and for the first time at the conference, the movement's many voices felt synced to the same beat. The silos cracked, and what emerged was a crescendo that negotiators could no longer ignore.

Not only does narrative power emerge from individual testimony, it builds when thousands of voices insist on standing by the same truth.

EQUITY AS A COLLECTIVE NARRATIVE

That kind of collective resonance is what drives the work of PolicyLink, placing equity at the center of policy design and advocating for a "Governing for All" agenda. For the purpose of this chapter, we'll use the definition of equity that means just and fair inclusion into a society where all can participate, prosper, and reach their full potential.[35]

Numbers can diagnose a problem, but stories make people care enough to fix it. PolicyLink's *Housing Justice Narrative Toolkit* is basically a plot-twist for the stale market-talk that usually

[35] "Equity vs Equality: Where It Differs (And How to Embrace Justice)," Embracing Equity, December 11, 2025, https://www.embracingequity.org/post/equity-vs-equality-where-it-differs-and-how-to-embrace-justice.

dominates housing debates. Instead of counting "housing units," the toolkit asks:

- What if we talk about *homes* instead of sterile square footage?
- What does *belonging* look like compared with a thin slice of "affordability"?
- How does framing stability as a matter of justice—rather than charity—flip the script?[36]

Picture a room full of policymakers who, instead of looking at charts, are listening to a single mother describe how she turns off the kitchen faucet at night to stretch a skyrocketing water bill. That image sticks far longer than a bar graph ever will.

In California, PolicyLink teamed up with the Alliance of Californians for Community Empowerment and the Right to the City Alliance to launch the "Homes for All" campaign. Instead of sprinkling statistics into city-council hearings, local organizers walked up to the podium armed with stories that felt like mini-movies:

- The kid who had to change schools every semester because the family's lease kept ending—each move erasing friendships and disrupting learning.
- The elderly neighbor who watched friends disappear from the same block after decades of living there, leaving empty porches that whispered "we used to be a community."
- The night-shift nurse who slept in her car between 12-hour shifts, dreaming of a roof she could finally call her own.

[36] "Housing Justice Narrative Toolkit," PolicyLink, accessed October 2025, https://www.policylink.org/sites/plorg/files/2025-07/Policylink_Housing_Justice_Toolkit_2-13.pdf.

Those anecdotes turned housing from a cold line item into the foundation of dignity. City councils in Richmond, Oakland, and Los Angeles responded with stronger tenant-protections and rent-stabilization ordinances. Because you can't ignore a story that hits home (literally).

PolicyLink has repeated this approach across issues. Their Transportation Equity Caucus, formed with the Leadership Conference on Civil and Human Rights, reframed transportation policy from a question of infrastructure to one of access. Highways, buses, and sidewalks became lifelines connecting people to jobs, schools, and healthcare. The stories shared by low-income commuters and disability advocates helped reframe transportation policy around access rather than infrastructure alone, informing how equity is discussed at the federal level.

Through their Water Equity and Climate Resilience Caucus, PolicyLink has worked with frontline communities to change how water policy is written, shifting from a narrow focus on cost to a rights-based framing that guarantees clean, safe, and affordable water for everyone. This initiative emerged alongside a broader coalition effort that culminated in California's 2012 Human Right to Water law.[37] The law's language reflected the stories PolicyLink and its partners had gathered. These accounts included mothers who turned off water taps to save money and families who relied on bottled water, despite living in one of the richest states in the country.

Across these movements, PolicyLink treats narrative as an organizing principle. They don't dictate messages; they

[37] Human Right to Water (HR2W) Portal, State Resources Control Board, California Water Boards, accessed January 14, 2026, https://www.waterboards.ca.gov/water_issues/programs/hr2w/.

convene storytellers—community leaders, advocates, artists, and researchers—to build shared frameworks that transcend single-issue silos. In recent years, federal housing and infrastructure guidance has increasingly reflected equity frameworks long advanced by organizations like PolicyLink.

VOICES THAT CHANGE THE RULES

If PolicyLink builds the scaffolding for collective equity, the Foundation for Individual Rights and Expression, better known as FIRE, shows how story can transform how a nation understands and defends free speech.[38] I think of the organization as the fire-fighter who rushes in with a megaphone, turning abstract legal battles into stories that people can picture in their minds.

Their work began on college campuses, where expression was often treated not as a right but as a privilege, bound by vague speech codes and political pressure.

Back in 2002, at Shippensburg University in Pennsylvania, a student filed a complaint after being told his political flyers violated the school's "speech zone" policy.

FIRE grabbed the story, splashed it across the media, and asked the obvious question: *Why does a university need a "speech zone" when the whole campus is supposed to be a marketplace of ideas?* Within months the university ripped up the restriction, and campuses nationwide started checking their own "speech zones" for any lingering relics of the past.

---

[38] Foundation for Individual Rights and Expression (FIRE), accessed October 2025, https://www.thefire.org.

In another case, a student newspaper tried to cover a controversial campus protest, only to discover that the university's budget office had suddenly "forgotten" to allocate funds for ink and paper. FIRE stepped in, turned the funding snub into a headline-making story about press freedom. Suddenly, this wasn't just about a missing check. It became a test of whether public universities truly uphold viewpoint-neutrality. The result? Several schools backed away from the intimidation tactics, and the student presses got their pens (and printers) back.

Fast forward to 2022. An art-history professor at Hamline University showed a 14th-century illustration of the Prophet Muhammad during a lecture on medieval iconography. The image sparked a heated debate, and the professor was dismissed.

FIRE lifted the case onto the national stage, framing it as a question of academic freedom rather than a niche art-history footnote. The conversation exploded across campuses, prompting scholars, students, and the public to wrestle with a delicate balance of respecting religious sensitivities while preserving the right to explore uncomfortable corners of history.

What ties these episodes together is how FIRE positions the disputes as human issues we can all recognize:

- Who gets to speak?
- Who decides what counts as acceptable speech?
- What happens when the volume knob is turned down?

When a student's flyer is boxed into a corner, when a campus newspaper's printer runs out of ink because someone doesn't like the story, or when a professor's slide triggers a campus-wide firestorm, the stakes become crystal-clear. These are cultural conversations exposing how fragile—and how vital—our right to speak up really is.

SHIFTING THE STORY OF FAIRNESS

In California, the tug-of-war over who pays and who benefits has impacted everything from school budgets to the streets where new homes rise or crumble. When voters approved Proposition 13 in 1978, the promise was to lock in low property taxes so homeowners could breathe easy.[39] What followed was a fiscal diet that left public services starving and widened the gap between rich and poor.

For decades, reformers tried to argue with spreadsheets. The math was sound, but the message was hollow. Californians were tired. They were tired of being told fairness could be calculated on a balance sheet. Then a new generation of community organizers—teachers, parents, small-business owners, and local leaders—decided to tell a different story. Working with groups like California Calls, the Million Voters Project, and PolicyLink, they built the "Schools and Communities First" campaign.[40] Instead of leading with percentages and loopholes, they talked about classrooms with forty students,

[39] "Common Claims About Proposition 13," Legislative Analyst's Office (LAO), September 19, 2016, https://lao.ca.gov/Publications/Report/3497.

[40] "Schools and Communities First Campaign," California Calls: Building Power for Working-Class Communities, accessed October 2025, https://www.cacalls.org.

Million Voters Project, accessed October 2025, https://www.millionvotersproject.org.

"Yes on Prop 15: Schools & Communities First Campaign," Power California, accessed October 2025, https://powercalifornia.org/scf.

clinics closing early, and potholes that never got fixed. They made the impact of Prop 13 personal.

The campaign reframed the issue from taxes to fairness. Its message highlighted that large corporations should pay property taxes at the same rate as the rest of us. Ads and town hall stories featured janitors, nurses, and small business owners who kept paying their share while corporate campuses sat on land taxed at 1970s values. The moral contrast was impossible to ignore.

Though the 2020 ballot initiative, Proposition 15, which sought to amend Proposition 13, fell just short of passing. Even so, it transformed the political terrain. Polling showed a major shift in public understanding. Californians began to see tax reform not as a threat, but as an investment in their neighbors and their children. Within two years, several counties implemented local versions of the proposal, and the state legislature introduced bills echoing the campaign's framing.

The real victory? A collective re-education of an entire state. Organizers forged a new narrative language that links revenue to community and shared responsibility.

* * *

THE NETWORK OF CHANGE

California's campaign was part of a much wider current. Across the country, a network of organizations has been doing similar work, changing not just *what* policies say, but *how* people understand them in the first place.

The Opportunity Agenda has long advanced the idea that cultural change precedes policy change. Their "Vision, Values, Voice" framework equips artists, advocates, and journalists to tell stories that link race, economy, and justice in ways data alone can't.[41] Years before criminal justice reform gained national momentum, they were helping communities talk about safety as opportunity. This language helped set the stage for sentencing reforms in states including New York and California.

Meanwhile, the Narrative Initiative trains movements to build shared story infrastructure across issues.[42] Their approach treats narrative like an ecosystem, a living system of stories, messengers, and metaphors that must be nourished if any movement is going to last.

The FrameWorks Institute takes a similar approach from a cognitive science perspective.[43] They test metaphors and framing to reveal how minds absorb complexity. Their research on "toxic stress," for example, changed how policymakers and journalists described early childhood development, helping move federal and state policy toward prevention, not punishment.

YOUR MIC CHECK

If you're organizing for systemic change, remember that no policy shifts without a chorus of voices. Storytelling at scale only works when people move to the same rhythm, carrying a shared beat of purpose.

---

[41] "Vision, Values, Voice: A Communications Toolkit," Opportunity Agenda, accessed October 2025, https://opportunityagenda.org/our-tools/communications-toolkit/.

[42] Narrative Initiative, accessed October 2025, https://www.narrativeinitiative.org.

[43] "Reframing Early Childhood Development and Learning," *Core Story Brief*, FrameWorks Institute, accessed October 2025, https://www.frameworksinstitute.org/app/uploads/2020/03/reframingearlychilddevelopment_alamancecounty.pdf.

1. **Challenge the Status Quo by Offering Solutions.** Real change begins when critique gives way to vision. Movements grow stronger when they imagine what comes next, including a new policy, a new system, a new story that turns injustice into design.
2. **Use the Power of Collective Action.** The most enduring stories are the ones echoed across movements—from "Later Is Too Late" at COP28 to "Schools and Communities First" in California. Each one reminds us that collective narrative comes through harmony. A movement becomes powerful when its voices align around shared values and visible demands.
3. **Speak to the Heart and the Head.** Data can persuade, but emotion mobilizes. Lead with lived experience. This can show up as the student in an overcrowded classroom, the mother rationing water, or the worker holding a paycheck that barely stretches. Anchor those stories in policy. Emotion opens the door; clarity keeps it open.
4. **Be Fearless in Your Authenticity.** Stories that change systems rarely land softly. They rattle rooms. They expose fault lines. They test our willingness to learn. The moments that make us uneasy often mark the edge of transformation. Step toward them.
5. **Amplify Marginalized Voices.** Equity means broadening who gets to tell the story. Seek out those whose voices have been sidelined and make space. A truly collective narrative doesn't just include; it redistributes who holds the mic.

TURN UP THE VOLUME

Turning a shared story into shared power takes more than passion. It requires structure. The organizers who transformed California's tax debate, the advocates who rallied the climate movement around "Later Is Too Late," and the networks that have spent decades training storytellers at PolicyLink, FIRE, and The Opportunity Agenda all know that strategy is what turns narrative into policy.

Make Your Message Vivid. The image of a student holding a handmade sign that reads *Our Classrooms Deserve Better* will outlast a stack of white papers. So will a worker describing the fear of a midnight raid or a nurse explaining why her clinic closed early.

Name the Structure. Every personal story carries a larger system behind it. Point to the backlog, the loophole, the policy gap. Make the invisible visible.

Pair the Story with an Ask. A story without direction is sentiment; a story with a goal is leverage. Always name the change you're asking for.

Protect the Storytellers. Visibility is not safety. Support the people who lend their lives to the public record. Make protecting them part of your campaign design.

Build the Rhythm. Movements grow when voices flow together, sung in the note everyone holds together.

THE DROP

Every movement begins as a murmur with a few people naming what others feel but haven't yet spoken. Over time, those murmurs find a shared beat, then harmony, then scale. That's how policy begins to bend.

At COP28, "Later Is Too Late" traveled through the halls like a pulse, passed from activist to diplomat to journalist until it became impossible to ignore. In California, organizers reframed a property tax law into a story about fairness and care. Across campuses, FIRE reminded the nation that free speech is the foundation of every other freedom and that democracy depends on dialogue, even when it's uncomfortable.

Each of these moments proves that when stories align around justice, they generate power greater than any single voice.

Policy is collective. It's written in the cadence of movements that refuse silence. And when those movements find their voice, the future listens.

6

THE STAGE IS NOT THE TABLE

Not everything that is faced can be changed,
but nothing can be changed until it is faced.

—James Baldwin

Every policy begins as a voice. But on the global stage, only a few microphones are turned on.

I was sharply reminded of this at COP16, the 2024 United Nations Biodiversity Conference in Cali, Colombia,[44] where governments, scientists, corporations, and civil society gathered to negotiate how the world will protect nature and biodiversity.

As I stood in a humid tent with the mountains of Cali calmly staring back at me and NGO leaders trading business cards, I was greeted by Alexandra Narvaez, Indigenous guard of the A'i Cofan community of Singango. This is someone celebrated across her

[44] "Sixteenth meeting of the Conference of the Parties to the Convention on Biological Diversity (COP 16)," Convention on Biological Diversity, updated February 27, 2025, https://www.cbd.int/conferences/2024.

region for defending her people's forests and fighting for the rights of women in her nation.

When I asked her what she thought of the gathering, its goals, and the whole scene, she smiled and took a deep breath.[45] She then sighed and slowly, almost imperceptibly, rolled her eyes. Her expression seemed to carry the weight of several past conferences. I recognized this instantly as the mix of exhaustion and determination that comes from showing up again and again, knowing the doors may still be closed, but refusing to stop knocking. That persistence itself is a kind of power, because the story doesn't end when the negotiations shut people out. It continues in the act of returning and refusing erasure.

Speaking in Spanish, she shared that while she and her fellow Indigenous leaders are grateful to be invited to these events, as it helps them gain visibility in support of protecting their land and ultimately getting land back, they're never invited to participate beyond the stage.

"This is my first time at COP, and there isn't much participation from Indigenous peoples. It seems that they (the organizers) do everything behind closed doors. Then they come out with a document, and we really don't have any say. The invitation the conference extends to us is simply to have us show up, but not to contribute to the negotiations."

To hold a global convening focused on how to protect the Earth's biodiversity without including Indigenous people—who steward 80 percent of the world's remaining ecosystems—in the decision-making process is like drafting a workplace harassment policy

[45] Melissa Jun Rowley, "Comment: For Indigenous peoples, failure to increase biodiversity finance is a matter of life or death," *Reuters*, December 5, 2024, https://www.reuters.com/sustainability/society-equity/comment-indigenous-peoples-failure-increase-biodiversity-finance-is-matter-life-2024-12-05/.

without talking to a single woman. It doesn't make sense to those of us who believe in justice. But it makes perfect sense to the powers that be.

"Is this conference one pretend, giant off-set?" I asked myself, recalling the disenchantment I felt months earlier during a different international climate action gathering. Not all of it was. Alongside the main event, a number of independent activations led by entrepreneurs, grassroots activists, climate tech innovators, and journalists put a spotlight on solutions made by the people, for the people.

But a stage and a seat at the table are not the same thing. I know it's easy to mistake visibility for influence, to think that because Indigenous voices spoke on panels they were also invited to agree on the outcomes. But they weren't. They were not invited to the negotiating room, and the absence of that invitation spoke a thousand words.

Stories have become a kind of currency in these spaces. They're swapped at conferences, leveraged in fundraising decks, and used to humanize data. Sometimes that exchange sparks action. If it gets the job done, meaning positive impact for the people in need, then I'm all for it. The issue is that far too often, this currency reduces people's lives to proof points for someone else's agenda.

During the rest of the conference, I learned of business leaders and diplomats praising the creation of the "Cali Fund," a voluntary mechanism to ensure biotech companies share DNA data revenues with Indigenous and local communities, a win worth celebrating. But when the applause faded, the numbers didn't add up. The fund was voluntary, the pledges small, and the financing far from the scale needed. Delegates from the Global South walked away frustrated, calling the commitments *"a drop in the sea."*

This gap between storytelling as power and storytelling as spectacle, transpires more often than not. In many instances, Indigenous and other frontline community leaders are invited to share their histories, their grief, and their vision for the future, only to have their words framed as atmosphere, not authority.

As they speak, the applause from the audience is real. The desire of onlookers to be a part of something meaningful and inclusive feels true. But what happens after that?

What's real beyond the mic drop?

Is storytelling being used to demand structural change, or simply to decorate the same broken systems with a new layer of public relations empathy?

Storytelling in justice movements must be measured by what follows the telling. A story is powerful when it creates space for new decisions, new alliances, and new accountability. Anything less risks turning lived experience into performance.

Too many campaigns collapse complex realities into one-note appeals designed to raise money or inspire guilt. Too many social media graphics smooth out the rough edges of human experience into bites that are easy to share and even easier to forget because there's only so much a post can do.

That doesn't mean stop posting. It means if the spirit moves you, look for the fuller story. It's out there. Look for whether or not it's being told where decisions are made. This includes in conversations that create budgets or in movements that travel beyond the scroll. Posts can spark awareness, but it's the deeper storytelling that keeps its edges, contradictions, and humanity that shifts what's possible.

Stories are knowledge. They carry frameworks for survival, blueprints for repair, and visions for futures that official documents don't even begin to outline. That's why storytelling in justice movements sometimes calls for handing over the microphone completely.

What I witnessed at COP16 made me think about the difference between a story and a narrative. Stories were shared, and they were powerful, personal, and full of truth. But the larger narrative of who holds authority and whose knowledge "counts" was already set by the structure of the gathering.

Image 5. Wider Guaramag, president of the A'i Cofán community of Sinangoe in Ecuador, me, Justin Piaguage, territorial leader of the Siekopai nation of Ecuador, and Alexandra Narvaez, Indigenous guard of the A'i Cofán community of Singangoe at COP16 in Cali, Colombia. October 2024.

* * *

STORIES VS. NARRATIVES

Stories are singular. They hold a voice, a moment, a truth. An Indigenous leader describing how her community guards forests. A farmer explaining how biodiversity sustains his family's harvest. A young activist sharing why she traveled across continents to speak on a stage.

Narratives are collective. They form when stories echo one another and accumulate until they shape how the world understands an issue. Narratives determine which truths are taken seriously, which are sidelined, and which are erased altogether.

The distinction is significant for justice. A story can move people in the moment, but a narrative dictates whether that story changes who gets invited into negotiations, who receives resources, and who is trusted as an authority. That's why those in power often allow stories but guard narratives. They'll applaud testimony from the stage, while keeping the master story, the one that defines who counts as an "expert," safely in their control.

At COP16, I saw this unfold like a stage play. Indigenous leaders told stories rooted in centuries of stewardship. Their words carried wisdom, ingenuity, and vision. But the narrative of decision-making authority remained with governments and corporations. The stories were present and flowing, while the narrative was locked and protected.

A story is a brick. The narrative is the architecture. This is the crux: stories can inspire, unsettle, or illuminate. Narratives decide whether those stories spark structural change or fade into spectacle. For movements seeking justice, the work is not only to tell stories but to contest narrative. This means pushing the frame wider and insisting that lived realities become central to the agreements, budgets, and policies that follow.

NARRATIVES OF THE DEEP

The debate over deep-sea mining reveals how systemic narratives are developed. For years, corporations and governments promoted it as an unavoidable step in the green transition, arguing that mining the seafloor for cobalt, nickel, and rare earth minerals was necessary to power clean energy technologies. The story leaned heavily on progress and inevitability, while sidelining the scale and permanence of the ecological damage beneath the surface.

In 2021, companies like Google, BMW, Volvo, and Samsung broke ranks with industry and publicly pledged they would not source minerals from the deep sea, joining World Wildlife Fund's (WWF) call for a moratorium on mining until its impacts could be better understood.[46] The following year, more than 600 scientists signed an open letter warning of catastrophic biodiversity loss if deep-sea mining went ahead unchecked. By 2023, at least twenty-one nations, from Pacific Island states to European governments, had aligned with those concerns, demanding either a ban or a pause while the International Seabed Authority (ISA) rushed to finalize regulations behind closed doors.[47]

[46] Helen Reid, "Google, BMW, AB Volvo, Samsung back environmental call for pause on deep-sea mining," *Reuters*, Updated March 31, 2021, https://www.reuters.com/business/sustainable-business/google-bmw-volvo-samsung-sdi-sign-up-wwf-call-temporary-ban-deep-sea-mining-2021-03-31/.

[47] Angeli Mehta, "Policy Watch: After fraught global meeting, future of deep-sea mining still hangs in balance," *Reuters*, updated August 4, 2023, https://www.reuters.com/sustainability/policy-watch-after-fraught-global-meeting-future-deep-sea-mining-still-hangs-2023-08-03/.

At the IUCN World Conservation Congress, thousands of delegates from governments, Indigenous groups, and NGOs voted to support a moratorium, calling the current pace of mining proposals "a drop in the sea" compared to the financing needed for real biodiversity protection.[48]

What shifted the debate wasn't new geology. It was new storytelling that included scientists showing fragile seafloor ecosystems, Indigenous leaders framing the ocean as kin, and corporations breaking the silence by refusing to buy in. Together, these stories began to dismantle the "inevitable progress" narrative and replace it with one rooted in responsibility and protection.

What happened in the fight against deep-sea mining reminds us that the way stories are told shapes narrative *and* outcomes. Power isn't limited to governments or corporations. It belongs to all of us.

This brings me to our next mic check—examinng the stories of injustice that we carry in our own lives?

YOUR MIC CHECK

The framework of voices invited to speak with lights, camera, and publicity all while decisions happen elsewhere doesn't only exist at global summits. It shows up in workplaces, schools, community meetings, news cycles, and even families. That said, in situations of injustice, while we don't always have the mic in our hands, we can notice where stories are positioned to land.

---

[48] Kanupriya Kapoor, "Conservation body calls for global moratorium on deep-sea mining," *Reuters*, September 8, 2021, https://www.reuters.com/business/environment/conservation-body-calls-global-moratorium-deep-sea-mining-2021-09-09/.

Think about a story of iniquity you've recently consumed. This could be a headline, a viral clip, a panel discussion, or a court appeal.

- Where was that story told?
- Who summarized what was said?
- Who was in the room when it ended?
- And what happened next?

In many spaces, stories are welcomed as testimony, but stopped short of influence. They are invited to be felt, not acted on—to inspire, not to decide.

So here's the check:

Was this story shared in a space of **visibility** or a space of **decision-making**?

Did the storyteller gain access, authority, or leverage? Or simply appreciation?

Were they invited back when budgets, language, or priorities were set?

Did the story alter who was trusted to speak next time?

Now widen the lens.

Where do *you* see this pattern repeating at work, in movements you're part of, or in institutions you move through? Where are stories circulating freely while dominant narratives remain tightly controlled?

Many people in these spaces do listen. The issue is around what happens to a story once it's been heard, who carries it forward, who translates it, and who decides what it's allowed to change.

TURN UP THE VOLUME

Justice-centered storytelling is a choice and a practice, one that can lead to shifts in power, not just attention. Here are ways to push further:

Audit Your Go-To Story. Choose a story you often tell about yourself or your work. Write it down. Then underline the parts you usually leave out. Ask: *If I included the failures, the contradictions, all the messy truths, how would the meaning shift?* The most effective stories hold paradox. They resist the instinct to sand down rough edges just to make things neater or more palatable.

Be Rigorous about Who Your Story Serves. Ask: *Does this story uphold the status quo, or does it question it? Does it simply invite sympathy, or does it demand accountability?*

Don't Confuse Amplification with Transfer of Power. It's one thing to give someone a platform. It's another to ensure their knowledge and vision influence the outcomes, policies, budgets, and priorities that follow. A thousand shares or standing ovations mean little if the structures harming them stay intact.

Flip the Frame. Before publishing a story, pause and ask: *Does this person appear as a symbol or a full human? Does this story build leverage for change or just momentary awareness?* If it's the latter, dig deeper.

Practice Discomfort. Justice stories are rarely tidy. Try resisting the urge to wrap yours up neatly. Let the rough edges show. Tell it in a way that leaves listeners unsettled and invite them to sit in that tension instead of rushing to resolution.

A Small Practice for Your Own Story. Write out a story you often use to introduce yourself. Then ask: *Where do I simplify to be relatable? What parts have I left out to protect myself or the audience's comfort? Who might be missing from this version? Whose influence, harm, or support gets erased? If I told it with nothing to prove, what would change?* The answers will point to where the real story lives.

Pass the Mic. In your next meeting, community gathering, or online post, amplify a voice that isn't usually heard—not by quoting them as inspiration, but by ensuring they have a say in the direction of the conversation. Remember, amplification isn't the same thing as transfer of power.

These practices help us develop our storytelling as disruption, re-centering, and accountability. Great storytelling in justice movements builds leverage, creates pressure, shifts resources, and reconfigures who is centered—not just in the narrative, but in the decisions, the funding streams, and the policies that follow.

THE DROP

Systems will not hand us justice. They are built to preserve power. But stories, when told truthfully, relationally, and with precision, can puncture those systems. They can shift who is heard and who gets to decide what happens next.

In the realm of justice, you are not obligated to tell stories that soothe anything. You have a right to tell stories that fully display complexities and redistribute attention and resources.

Your story—messy, layered, inconvenient—is not just yours. It is a thread in a much larger weave of collective memory and future possibility. And when you speak it with honesty, you don't just resist erasure. You ignite the possibility of a more just world.

Fairness isn't created in conference halls or polished press releases. It is built every time we the people refuse to let a story serve as a mere decoration and instead become a demand.

7

BUSINESS, STORY, AND LEGACY

Great brands aren't built on what they sell, but on the stories they tell—and the purpose they serve.

—Adapted from Seth Godin

Many lives ago, I was newly hired as a production assistant at CNN Business News, logging stock tickers and editing the top headlines that were moving markets. At every opening bell, the trading floor of the New York Stock Exchange erupted like the craps tables in Las Vegas. Voices roared, hands flew into the air, papers flew everywhere. Whoever landed in the green or red at the closing bell could make or break an entire country's mood because the numbers were never just numbers. Every uptick or crash evoked a story of power.

That was the first time I understood that money is never neutral. Every dollar tells a story about the future it fuels, whose vision gets funded, whose risks are forgiven, and whose labor is undervalued. Years later, when I became a tech and business reporter, I began to see that same pattern play out on a global scale. Money continued to shape markets and meaning, defining who and what modern society valued in the process. Over time, I realized that companies were culture movers, turning consumer values into strategy and public trust into currency.

Case in point: between 2013 and 2017, a new trend emerged in the corporate world. While selling products, brands were staking out positions on social issues. CEOs, once expected to stay neutral, began sounding less like cautious executives and more like statesmen.

Across fashion, tech, retail, and finance, business leaders were stepping into political debates on immigration bans, LGBTQ+ rights, racial justice, and climate. A 2016 *Harvard Business School* analysis noted the growing phenomenon of "CEO activism,"[49] and by 2017, the term had entered mainstream media. The public began to expect corporations to show up, not just in the marketplace, but in civic life.

The Fashion Revolution movement was born in 2013 after the Rana Plaza factory collapse in Bangladesh.[50] Within a year, campaigns like *#WhoMadeMyClothes* pushed brands to confront their supply chains, setting a new expectation that business was accountable for human rights, not just profits.

Starbucks attempted to wade into racial justice with its 2015 "Race Together" campaign, inviting baristas to spark conversations

---

[49] Carmen Nobel, "When CEOs Become Activists," *Working Knowledge*, Harvard Business School, April 20, 2016, https://www.library.hbs.edu/working-knowledge/when-ceos-become-activists.

Aaron "Ronnie" Chatterji and Michael W. Toffel, "The New CEO Activists," *Harvard Business Review*, January–February 2018, https://hbr.org/2018/01/the-new-ceo-activists.

[50] Fashion Revolution, accessed November 15, 2025, https://www.fashionrevolution.org/about/.

on racial inequality by writing the phrase on coffee cups. This was widely criticized as clumsy and performative.[51] Yet Starbucks didn't retreat from the issue. Instead, it shifted its narrative to one grounded in employee values, investing in racial-bias training for 175,000 staff members and creating long-term equity initiatives.

This marked a cultural turning point. A Fortune 500 company acknowledged that racial inequality was not only a civic issue, but a business concern. Despite its missteps, the campaign revealed how unavoidable and risky it had become for brands to not speak on issues of justice.

When the global refugee crisis captured headlines in 2015, several companies used their platforms to advocate for compassion and inclusion. Airbnb launched its Open Homes initiative to provide free housing for displaced families.[52] Ikea designed modular shelters for refugee camps. Both efforts showed how business could function as a force for dignity, reminding the world that design and innovation don't mean much if they don't serve people.

The effect led to a cultural shift, carving out space for companies to discover that their brand story was inseparable from their position on social and political events. A brand's legacy wasn't defined only by what it sold, but by what it was willing to defend.

---

[51] Connor Friedersdorf, "Overcaffeinated on the Starbucks 'Race Together' Campaign," *The Atlantic*, March 18, 2015, https://www.theatlantic.com/business/archive/2015/03/overcaffeinated-attacks-on-the-starbucks-race-together-campaign/388072/.

[52] "Airbnb.org expands temporary housing support for refugees," Airbnb Newsroom, June 20, 2024, https://news.airbnb.com/airbnb-org-expands-temporary-housing-support-for-refugees/.

THE COST VS. THE GAIN

Some of these corporate stands came at a cost. Campaigns misfired. Boycotts erupted. Commentators accused brands of "virtue signaling." But there was value in all of this, as companies used storytelling to absorb backlash, clarify their values, and build credibility over time.

A clear example is Nike's 2018 partnership with Colin Kaepernick. The "Dream Crazy" campaign centered on a stark black-and-white ad featuring Kaepernick's face and a single line of text that said: "*Believe in something. Even if it means sacrificing everything.*" The message directly referenced his decision to kneel during the national anthem in protest of racial injustice and police violence.

The response to the ad was immediate and polarized. Critics filmed themselves burning Nike shoes. Calls for boycotts spread across social media. Cable news framed the campaign as reckless and divisive. But Nike did not retreat. Instead, the company continued running the ad, featuring Kaepernick prominently across its platforms, and aligning the campaign with its broader brand identity around risk, conviction, and performance. The gamble worked. Nike's sales surged, and its brand deepened loyalty with the very consumers it wanted to reach.[53]

The point wasn't to be appealing to everyone. It was to deepen loyalty with the people who shared their values. This included the customers, employees, and communities who would carry the brand forward.

---

[53] Soo Youn, "Nike sales booming after Colin Kaepernick ad, invalidating critics," *ABC News*, December 21, 2018, https://abcnews.go.com/Business/nike-sales-booming-kaepernick-ad-invalidating-critics/story?id=59957137.

THE AGE OF CORPORATE BACKPEDALING

By 2025, the landscape started to look drastically different. The flood of CEO statements we saw a decade earlier has slowed to a trickle. Today, while some companies are gradually making safe statements about the importance of peace in US cities amid horrific ICE raids, most companies are quieter, more cautious, wary of political and legal backlash. Entire diversity teams have been dissolved. Corporate equity programs have been scaled back or abandoned. Longstanding commitments once touted as bold examples of values-driven leadership are being quietly rewritten or erased.

In some circles, there are valid reasons for this. Fear and apprehension around lawsuits, shareholder activism, and political rhetoric have made values-driven positions count more (to some) as risks rather than responsibilities. For many business leaders, what once felt like an inevitable shift toward solidarity and shared accountability now feels like contested ground.

And yet, even as many brands pull back, others continue to stand firm. In 2025, Delta Air Lines reiterated that "DEI is about talent," resisting the push toward neutrality. At the same time, Costco drew strong support from its board and shareholders, rejecting anti-DEI resolutions and affirming the value of inclusion.

On the activist side, Ben & Jerry's filed a federal lawsuit against its parent company Unilever in 2025, alleging that Unilever was silencing its public statements in support of Palestinian refugees.[54]

[54] Jessica DiNapoli and Jonathon Stempel, "Ben & Jerry's accuses Unilever of muzzling it because of Trump," *Reuters*, January 27, 2025, https://www.reuters.com/legal/ben-jerrys-accuses-unilever-muzzling-it-because-trump-2025-01-24.

The dynamics are anything but black and white. Some companies including Costco, Cisco, Microsoft, and Apple continue to hold their ground on DEI. Yet at the same time, Microsoft's co-founder Bill Gates and Apple's CEO Tim Cook[55] maintain close ties with an administration that openly opposes those very commitments. And for audiences, employees, customers, and communities, the gap between what companies say and who they align with has never been more visible.

Every company working within capitalism is extractive in some way. To produce anything means to draw from resources—human, environmental, or both. No one living in modern society is separate from this. I'm writing this book on my laptop, made by Apple, and it will be printed using paper, ink, and energy that create their own carbon footprints. During my book tour, I'll travel to locations in the US and across the globe to promote my work, creating more carbon footprints.

The question isn't whether or not grayness is inevitable; of course it is. The question is how much capacity and willingness we, as consumers and as brands, have to align our choices with our values as closely as possible. What compromises do we accept, and which do we refuse? What legacy do we want to leave through our actions?

Jessica DiNapoli, "Ben & Jerry's calls war in Gaza a 'genocide,'" *Reuters*, May 29, 2025, https://www.reuters.com/world/middle-east/unilevers-ben-jerrys-calls-war-gaza-genocide-2025-05-29.

Jessica DiNapoli, "Ben & Jerry's says parent Unilever silenced it over Gaza stance." *Reuters*, updated November 14, 2024, https://www.reuters.com/business/retail-consumer/ben-jerrys-says-parent-unilever-silenced-it-over-gaza-stance-2024-11-14.

[55] "Apple's Tim Cook says he's proud to be gay," *The Express Tribune*, October 14, 2024, https://tribune.com.pk/story/783541/apples-tim-cook-says-proud-to-be-gay.

In the end, much of this comes down to our narratives, which consist of the stories we choose to tell about what we made, how we made it, and who it served.

* * *

The greatest human stories often revolve around personal transformation, in a person facing a challenge, growing through it with guts and glory, and emerging forever changed. Brand stories at their best follow the same arc. They may come from a business changing how an industry operates or a leader reimagining the terms of a market itself.

That's what struck me in my conversation with Denise Cherry, Head of Marketing at Rivian, at SXSW in 2025. The discussion was less about cars and more about people and how an automaker can drive a broader transformation in energy and community. Rivian, one of the most successful challengers to the old auto giants, isn't only known for its sleek trucks and SUVs. Its story is rooted in accelerating the clean energy transition, building not only vehicles but also the charging networks, supply chains, and partnerships that make decarbonization possible.

Through a storytelling lens, we talked about why inclusivity in the clean energy transition is the only way it will work and how companies can make their commitments resonate beyond glossy reports. Climate strategies aren't worth much if people can't experience them in their communities.

The most powerful brand narratives aren't based on technical specs or carbon metrics. They're made of stories showcasing real-world examples of tangible change reaching real people in ways they can feel in their daily lives.

That same thread ran through my conversations with Aileen Lerch of Allbirds and Stephan Jacob of Cotopaxi at the Carbon Newbie Summit during SF Climate Week. Both companies have built their reputations on proving that sustainability and style can work as one.

Allbirds has turned regenerative wool, plant-based leathers, and natural materials into the foundation of a global footwear brand that speaks to both comfort and conscience. Cotopaxi, with its bright apparel and "Gear for Good" mantra, has woven ethics into every seam—from fair labor practices to community reinvestment in the regions where its products are made.

Listening to Lerch and Jacob, it was clear that their story-engine lives in the communities behind their products. When you buy a pair of Allbirds shoes or a Cotopaxi backpack, you're supporting a narrative about fairness, innovation, and the possibility of doing business more equitably.

BEYOND THE BOTTOM LINE

While I was living in Beirut, Lebanon a decade ago, I saw the same storytelling principles at work in ventures born out of necessity and imagination. My experience in Beirut can be summed up in four words: resilience is a lifestyle.

In those years, Lebanon's startup scene was defying expectations. Power outages were daily. The internet was slow. And the country hosted more than a million refugees. Yet, inside hubs like Beirut Digital District (BDD), ideas were flowing faster than the current. At the time, BDD's workforce was majority female—an inversion of nearly every Western tech ecosystem. Young developers like Asia Joumaa, who graduated at the top of the coding bootcamp

SE Factory, were proving that talent and determination can out-code circumstances.

These women were writing a story of innovation from which I believe startup ecosystems around the world—including Silicon Valley—could have learned.[56] They weren't chasing unicorn valuations; they were building solutions for communities under strain.

That same ethos ran through startups such as Proximie, founded by Dr. Nadine Hachach-Haram, which used augmented-reality technology to let surgeons guide operations remotely in conflict zones. Others like Sensio Air, Play My Way, and MakerBrane combined engineering and empathy, addressing public-health gaps, education barriers, and creative expression. In northern Lebanon, Najwa Sahmarani and Fadi Mikati launched the Tripoli Entrepreneurs Club, turning a city once scarred by sectarian violence into a place where startups could outgrow despair.

During that time, a new financing policy called Circular 331 began injecting hundreds of millions of dollars into Lebanon's knowledge economy, catalyzing venture funds and angel networks. But what struck me most wasn't the capital. It was the mindset. As one founder in Tripoli told me, "No one is as serious as the entrepreneurs here because we have the survival needs."

Those words stayed with me. In Lebanon, entrepreneurship didn't stem from the desire to create disruption or secure dominance. It came from the need to cultivate *staying power*. Many pitch decks carried an unspoken question: How can we build something that keeps our community standing when everything else feels like it's falling apart?

---

[56] Melissa Jun Rowley, "What Silicon Valley Can Learn from Lebanon's Women in Tech," *TechCrunch*, June 6, 2017, https://techcrunch.com/2017/06/06/what-silicon-valley-can-learn-from-lebanons-women-in-tech/.

I worked with several founders to explore how businesses that weren't traditionally "impact-first" could still bake purpose into their operations. These included cafés sourcing ingredients from local farmers, small fashion brands ensuring fair wages, software firms measuring their carbon footprints. The shift was operational *and* narrative. Their business stories expanded beyond *what* they sold to *why* they existed, and those stories became magnets for investors and partners who might otherwise have looked away.

YOUR MIC CHECK

Whether you run a company, work inside one, invest in one, or simply choose where your money goes, you're already participating in business storytelling. Every purchase, pitch, hiring decision, or partnership reinforces a narrative about what and whom is assigned worth. You don't need a title or a board seat to influence that story. You're already in the room.

Think about the brands you trust, the ones you recommend without being asked. What first drew you in? What made that connection stick?

Through your everyday choices—what you support, question, push back on, or step away from—you're already participating in which business stories gain momentum and which ones fade. Some decisions are conscious. Others happen through habit or convenience. All of them add up.

Legacy in business is built through repeated decisions that either consolidate power or redistribute it, extract value or return it, and preserve the status quo or push it to evolve.

The invitation here is to notice where your attention goes as consumer, investor, or business owner.

That awareness is agency. And agency is authorship.

TURN UP THE VOLUME

Ways to practice justice-centered storytelling in business and consumer choices this week:

- **Ask for the Receipts.** Founders: back your claims with evidence. Don't just say "carbon-neutral" or "inclusive." Show the data, the policies, the partnerships that make it real. Consumers: demand that transparency and reward it when you see it.
- **Elevate Local Voices.** If you're building a company, highlight the workers, suppliers, and communities that sustain you. If you're a customer, share those stories when you see them done well.
- **Reward Resilience.** Whether you're buying or building, support the businesses that hold steady even under pressure—those that keep policies designed for equity alive, that commit to sustainable sourcing even when costs rise, and that don't abandon values when challenged.

THE DROP

When I think back to the NYSE trading floor—the roar, the frenzy, the flashes of red and green—I understand that every movement on that screen was a mirror of belief. Markets are collective acts of storytelling. They rise and fall on performance, but even more on perception about what we choose to value, protect, and repeat.

Every stock surge, every layoff, and every campaign tells a story about who we think deserves abundance and who is expected to survive on scarcity. For decades, those stories were told almost exclusively by the powerful boards, the billionaires, and brand strategists who decided what good business looked like.

That's changing. The most significant storytellers in business today aren't just CEOs with microphones. They're the employees, customers, and communities holding companies accountable to their words. They're the people demanding that the story line up with fairness.

The old story of business dictated growth at any cost. The new story asks growth, for what purpose, and for whom. The companies that will thrive next are the ones that understand that trust is capital and transparency is currency. Their balance sheets measure more than profit. They measure participation. They invest in values not because it's fashionable, but because it's the only sustainable model left.

Compelling corporate storytelling is human-centered and shares how employees and customers are impacted by policies, pay equity, and carbon footprints. It's transparent about who gets to sit at the table when decisions are made, and it turns mission statements into measurable change.

Business has always been a mirror of humanity. When it tells a better story, so can we. Rivian, Allbirds, Cotopaxi, and the founders I met in Beirut are not outliers. They're early authors of a new narrative—one where creativity, conscience, and commerce can coexist. They remind us that innovation without empathy isn't progress. It's performance.

We all take part in this story through every purchase, every investment, and every moment of attention that becomes a sentence in the ongoing draft of our shared economy.

So the question becomes, what kind of narrative are we the people funding? Eventually, the market reflects more than numbers. It reflects character.

The stories that endure are written beyond headlines and quarterly reports. They appear in the lives touched along the way. They belong to the people and companies who refuse to treat business as neutral, the entrepreneurs who choose integrity over image, and the innovators who believe that capitalism, when stripped of its illusions, can still be a vessel for good.

The story you tell through what you build, fund, support, and choose is a legacy you leave behind. And it's yours to carry forward with clarity, imagination, and resolve.

PART 3

LANDING THE BRIDGE

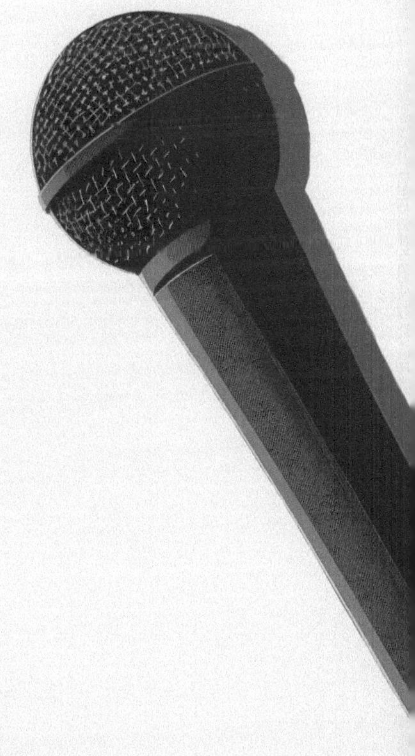

8

THE GRAMMAR OF EMOTION: WHY WE REACH OUR GREATEST POWER WHEN WE DIVE INTO OUR DEEPEST VULNERABILITY

What is most personal is most universal.

—Carl Rogers, *On Becoming a Person*

Two hundred pairs of expectant eyes locked into mine as I stood on stage in Casablanca. I was about to deliver a keynote address to young women entrepreneurs from across the Middle East and North Africa, a region that had become a second home to me. The air smelled of salt and mint tea, and outside, the call to prayer wafted through the city. I had a microphone in hand and a choice to make—to either deliver the safe, data-heavy keynote I'd written, or speak from the scar instead of the script.

For years, I had made a career out of elevating other people's voices, while keeping my own stories hidden behind bylines and my default mode of interviewing people on the spot. I'll never forget the day I reunited with a former boyfriend after several months of not speaking.

"Melissa, stop interviewing me," he said, ten minutes into our conversation.

"Oh, am I doing that?" I asked. "Do I do that a lot?"

"Yes, of course, you do," he said smiling. "It's part of your inquisitive charm. But today, let's just be here and connect. Tell me how you're feeling. Tell me a story, something personal." I didn't know where or how to begin.

That's the thing about making a living out of telling other people's stories. It's easy to forget how to tell your own—at least it had been for me—until that day in Casablanca.

It wasn't that I didn't understand emotions. I mean, I knew how to interview for emotional resonance, how to package inspiration into a remarkable but believable shape, and how to massage trauma into something audiences could consume but not have to carry.

What I hadn't learned was how to tell the unvarnished truth about my own professional failures and messes—the layoffs, the burnouts, the months spent living on my best friend's couch, wondering if I'd ever earn enough money to afford paying rent again.

Standing on that stage in front of those women, some of whom had put their own lives on the line to build a business, I realized the grammar of emotion is more than an accessory to a story. It's the reason for telling any story worth telling. It's what makes people lean forward instead of turn their heads down and doomscroll. It's what makes us all feel seen and understood.

So I closed my laptop, ditched my slides, and spoke off the cuff.

I spoke about being laid off three times in seven years, "due to the economy." I told them about the humiliation of the dot-com crash and the trauma of the 2008 recession. I shared moments of panic over clients who ghosted on paying invoices the same week my rent was due. I talked about my depression, the numbness I was too disembodied to fully notice, and the burnout I normalized. I even talked about the times I nearly gave up on being a writer altogether, until a friend pointed out that the storytelling skills I was so quick to dismiss were exactly what business leaders needed.

The energy in the room shifted, as it became clear that the women in the audience weren't simply listening to me. They were feeling with me. Some nodded and gave knowing smiles. Others leaned forward like they'd been holding their breath and could finally exhale. My story wasn't extraordinary. It was just honest. And that honesty made space for others to show up more fully in their own.

STORIES AS BLUEPRINTS FOR SURVIVAL

After I spoke, women entrepreneurs from across the Middle East and North Africa took the stage one by one, sharing their business plans and, most importantly, their "why."

One had launched a childcare collective to support working mothers. Another created a job-training program for refugees. One woman was tackling deforestation with community-led conservation projects. These startups were lifelines woven from lived experience and vision.

And then came Yara Yassin.

Yara, co-founder of the Cairo-based startup Up-Fuse, stood with calm conviction as she told the story of transforming plastic waste into upcycled products while providing dignified jobs for local artisans.[57] What started as a design-school question—*How can we turn waste into something beautiful?*—had become a company grounded in sustainability, creativity, and economic justice.

The emotional grammar of her pitch went beyond the story of a lifestyle brand—beyond the mic drop. What Yara shared was a story of what's possible when we stop waiting for permission and start creating from purpose. And that's what won her the competition.

What stayed with me long after the applause faded was the reminder that every person in that room shared a deeply personal story, a journey of self-discovery and transformation.

In the screenwriting book *The Anatomy of Story: 22 Steps to Becoming a Master Storyteller*, John Truby devotes much of his storytelling framework to how a protagonist must change.[58] Whether it's from weakness to strength, disillusionment to purpose, fear to courage, or, like Yara, taking a problem and turning it into a solution, every main character must experience the journey of transformation for a story to sell.

For me, transformation that day in Casablanca unfolded when I stopped worrying about what I thought people wanted to hear and shared what I'd been longing to say.

That takes diving into an unfamiliar level of vulnerability. It takes getting raw and naked as truth. That's the grammar of emotion.

---

[57] "Yara Yassin," Creative Ind MENA, accessed November 15, 2025, https://creativeindmena.com/speaker/yara-yassin/.

[58] John Truby, *The Anatomy of Story: 22 Steps to Becoming a Master Storyteller* (Faber & Faber, 2007).

Image 6. On the left, Yara Yassin, co-founder and design director of the Egyptian startup Up-fuse, stands next to two smiling workers who hold up a sign that reads "I made your bag." In April, Yara and her co-founder Rania Rafle took home $50,000 for winning first place in the *#WeMENA* Challenge, a *#business* competition created by the World Bank, Voyaj, and YouNoodle. April 2017.

BHUTAN: A RELATIONSHIP WITH 'ENOUGH'

Months later, as I continued on this path, encountering remarkable humans defying the odds stacked against them, I found myself sitting cross-legged on the polished wood floor of Dodeydra Monastery, high in the Himalayas, across from Bhutan's third-highest-ranking monk. Outside, the air smelled of pine and wild rivers. Inside, it was startlingly quiet until the meditation began.

After five minutes of chanting with a room full of monks and rinpoches,[59] who gave my traveling companions and me a lifelong blessing, voices rose in unison, vibrating together. It felt as if the chant might lift the entire room off the mountain.

I could hardly imagine the commitment it must take to become a monk. The juxtaposition of me, someone who couldn't manage to reside in a city for more than 1.5 years at a time, next to a dozen men who had dedicated their lives to stillness and service, was almost absurd. Yet as I sat there, legs numb, lungs syncing with their chants, I felt peace and surrender. These men had chosen constancy in a world built on motion. I had chosen motion in search of meaning. For a moment, both paths met in the same breath.

I had come to Bhutan hoping to understand how the country measures Gross National Happiness instead of GDP and how they had made well-being the centerpiece of their national identity.[60]

One of the monks told me it wasn't really about "happiness," at least not the way we lunge after it in the West. It wasn't about adrenaline, novelty, or dopamine either. It was about contentment, a kind of emotional steadiness rooted in interdependence

---

[59] Tibetan term meaning "precious one," an honorific title for revered Buddhist teachers.

Damien Keown, ed., "Rinpoche," *Oxford Dictionary of Buddhism*, Oxford University Press, 2013.

[60] *Constitution of the Kingdom of Bhutan*, Royal Government of Bhutan, 2008, https://www.constituteproject.org/constitution/Bhutan_2008.

Karma Ura, et al., *An Extensive Analysis of GNH Index*, Centre for Bhutan Studies and GNH Research, 2012.

with family, community, the forest, and building a solid foundation for future generations.

"Contentment is deeper than happiness," he said, his voice as gentle as the saffron robes pooled around him. "It is a relationship with enough."

Bhutan's entire story is built around that notion. It's why the country passes laws that protect biodiversity over business, why their forests are sacred spaces rather than resources to be strip-mined, and why climate legislation is framed as a moral imperative. Their national narrative doesn't simply inspire contentment. It requires it, and the country's policies flow directly from that emotionally grounded architecture.

As I listened, I realized he wasn't just describing a feeling. He was outlining a framework. Bhutan had written contentment into its national identity, and from that story every law and policy unfolded.[61] It made me think about how every country, every movement, every brand, and every person lives inside a narrative of their own making.

Many other governments build their narratives around security, or supremacy, or profit, or growth at all costs. Whatever story gets told most consistently becomes the grammar and syntax of daily life, influencing decisions, feelings, desires, even what people dare to imagine.

If you want to shift that story—whether to change a single mind, redirect a community's priorities, or alter a nation's trajectory—you can't begin with metrics or raw facts. Real transformation starts with feeling, because a narrative must be experienced before it can be measured.

---

[61] Karma Ura and Karma Galay, *Gross National Happiness and Development: Proceedings of the First International Seminar on Operationalization of Gross National Happiness*, Centre for Bhutan Studies, 2004. See speech by Jigme Singye Wangchuck, "Gross National Happiness," 1972.

Image 7. The opening ceremony at Dodeydra Monastery in Thimphu, Bhutan. November 2018.

Image 8. A few minutes before meditation began at Dodeydra Monastery in Thimphu, Bhutan. November 2018.

THE MYTH OF RATIONAL PERSUASION

None of us are emotionally moved by spreadsheets. We're moved by how it feels to be alive, to be fragile, to be connected to something bigger. This is the human current flowing beneath every story that has ever shifted culture or policy or the intimate landscape of someone's heart.

For decades, we were taught to believe that if we simply laid out the right facts in the right order, people would come to the right conclusions. We were taught that truth, if offered cleanly enough, would speak for itself.

But the brain doesn't work that way. And the human heart has never taken orders from a pie chart.

Neuroscience shows that emotions play a crucial role in decision-making. Antonio Damasio's research[62] revealed that patients with damage to the emotional centers of the brain could reason through choices with perfect logic, but could not actually make decisions. The absence of emotion left them paralyzed.

It turns out that emotion isn't the enemy of reason. It's the precondition for it.

Our brains process emotional input milliseconds before logic kicks in. When someone hears a story, their amygdala lights up before their prefrontal cortex can engage. We feel before we think. And if a story doesn't register emotionally, it may never register at all.

---

[62] Ed Batista, "Antonio Damasio on Emotion and Reason," *Ed Batista Executive Coach blog*, July 31, 2011, https://edbatista.com/2011/07/antonio-damasio-on-emotion-and-reason.html.

Antonio Damasio, *Descartes' Error: Emotion, Reason and the Human Brain* (Penguin, 2005).

UNDERSTANDING THE BACKFIRE EFFECT

This is why advocates and journalists often encounter the *Backfire Effect*: when people presented with information that contradicts their beliefs become even more entrenched in those beliefs.

It doesn't matter how solid the evidence is. If the information feels like a threat, it triggers fight-or-flight. Survival mode doesn't make space for nuance. But a personal story, such as a neighbor who got sick or a wildfire that burned down someone's hometown, can break through. Not because it's perfectly sourced, but because it's human.

Facts aren't persuasive on their own. They need a story to hold them and a feeling to propel them forward.

CHANGING CLIMATE POLICY WITH ONE PANTHER

In 2021, the Florida Wildlife Corridor Act passed with rare bipartisan support. It wasn't driven by data-heavy lobbying. It was supported by the documentary *Path of the Panther.*[63]

The film followed conservation photographer Carlton Ward Jr. as he tracked Florida's elusive panther across fragmented habitats. The narrative was built on the intimacy of one animal struggling to survive in a shrinking world.

The panther became more than a species. It became a metaphor: for loss, for beauty, for what's left when we don't act in time.

When lawmakers saw the film, their emotional response was immediate. What data hadn't moved for years, a story moved in under ninety minutes.

[63] *The Path of the Panther*, Eric Bendick, dir. (National Geographic, 2023).

The Architecture of Emotion

Think of storytelling like architecture:

- Emotion is the foundation.
- Relatability is the entry point.
- Facts are the framing.
- And the ask—the change, the belief, the action—is the window you open at the end.

If you skip the foundation and start hammering facts together, you might build something that looks solid, but no one will want to walk inside.

That's why we remember cracks in voices more than charts and why we forget numbers but remember the trembling, the silence, and the story.

THE POWER OF METAPHOR

Metaphors define how we experience reality.

Climate change framed as a "time bomb" suggests urgency. As "slow-moving," it risks apathy. As "a fever," it opens the door to healing.

Words aren't neutral. They carry values, assumptions, and worldviews. If we're not deliberate, we reinforce the very systems we're trying to change.

Think of "Flatten the curve" at the start of COVID-19. Those three words and one simple graph turned an abstract threat into a communal act of protection. It wasn't epidemiology that went viral. It was a story of solidarity.

LEAD WITH EMOTION. FOLLOW WITH TRUTH. END WITH CLARITY

Here's the rhythm:

1. **Start with a Spark.** Give an emotional anchor.
2. **Build the Bridge.** Use metaphors, shared values, and familiar images.
3. **Introduce the Shift.** Bring forward the change, the tension, the new lens.
4. **Ground It in Meaning.** Bring in the fact that sharpens the point.
5. **Close with a Window.** Leave the audience with an opening, not a wall.

When you tell stories this way, you do more than inform. You transform.

FINAL THOUGHT: SPEAK HUMAN, NOT JUST SMART

We live in an age where truth is debated, distorted, and drowned. But there's one truth that cuts through every time, and that's how it feels to be human.

Your task as a storyteller is to carry truth in a vessel people are willing to open. To build stories not just with facts, but with feeling. To speak, always, in the grammar of emotion.

YOUR MIC CHECK

You know those flickers of ideas that show up out of nowhere, the ones that tap at your attention while you're brushing your teeth or half-listening to a conversation? Those are gentle nudges to start something, to write something, and finally say the thing that keeps circling in your mind that you haven't been able to name.

It's easy to think of these moments as interruptions or distractions. But what if they're invitations to tell your story? Writing down the whisper of an idea or experience that won't leave you in a notebook, a voice memo, or a half-finished document can help you create an elegant kind of authorship over your own life. This is a way of choosing presence and grace for yourself rather than continuing to spin.

The stories that stay with us aren't always the tidy, sunny tales. They're often the moments or episodes filled with uncertainty, discomfort, or a desire we're not sure how to articulate. Sometimes, these stories feel embarrassing, tender, or sore. So it's no wonder we might not want to face them, let alone share them with anyone else.

What's beautifully human about these stories is they have a pulse. We can't get rid of them because they're moving inside of us wanting a way out. When we give ourselves permission to tell stories like this without polishing away the edges, we shift from being characters caught inside events we can't control to observers and authors with agency.

There's a spacious, neutral feeling that emerges when we're no longer simply reacting to what happens, and instead noticing how an experience lands and what it stirs inside us. That act of presence alone is a form of authorship. And that's you taking back your power.

TURN UP THE VOLUME

This kind of attention doesn't require an audience. It often begins in private—in a notebook, on a long walk, in a conversation where you decide to speak one sentence more honestly than you had planned. The volume rises not because you push it, but because you stop muting yourself. You let your imperfections fly free.

Start with moments that linger, the exchanges that follow you around. These could be conversations you replay on the drive home, reactions that surprise you, silences that feel heavier than they should. Those are usually signals.

Instead of asking, *What's the message?* try asking, *What stayed with me? Was it discomfort? Relief? Shame? Relief followed by shame?* The emotional sequence matters more than the explanation.

When you write or speak from those places, resist the instinct to clean them up. Let the contradiction stay. Let the uncertainty show. Most people don't recognize themselves in polished conclusions. They see themselves in the moment before clarity arrives.

And don't rush to make meaning. Meaning comes later. First comes noticing, naming, and sitting long enough with the experience that it stops performing and starts revealing.

You'll know you're close when the story feels slightly risky to tell, not because it's dramatic, but because it's true.

That's where resonance begins.

THE DROP

Stories don't ask to be perfect. They ask to be told while they're still alive.

When you stay with imperfection long enough, a story stops being an object you present and becomes a place you stand. From there, you're no longer performing an experience. You're inhabiting it. The power to reach people thrives in the willingness to remain present with what's unfinished.

You don't need a conclusion to speak honestly. You don't need permission to name what moved you or unsettled you or stayed with you long after the moment passed. You only need to notice when something inside you asks for attention and to answer it without rushing past.

This is how stories deepen rather than perform. This is how meaning accumulates without being forced.

When you stop chasing the right words and start trusting the ones that arrive, and when you stop trying to impress and start allowing yourself to be seen, people recognize themselves because you showed them how it felt to be human. That's the grammar of emotion.

9

THE ETHICS OF STORYTELLING IN A POLARIZED WORLD: NAVIGATING THE THIN LINE BETWEEN ADVOCACY, MISINFORMATION, AND PROPAGANDA

In the age of rampant algorithms and convenient echo chambers, stories sprint through our days and occasionally set themselves on fire. They lay the groundwork for who ends up being believed, who gets targeted, who receives resources, and who wakes up trending for reasons that may ruin your breakfast.

A single caption can rally a city. A rumor can move markets. A clipped video of two co-workers cuddling on a jumbotron can end a career. At the same time, a testimony can pass a bill, and a community archive can protect a neighborhood. In this era, the distance between a post uploaded from someone's bed or bathroom and a national consequence has shrunk to seconds.

This is the terrain many of us are navigating now. And it's uneven and noisy, with hidden caves where context collapses and consequences echo long after the moment has passed.

WHEN STORIES OUTRUN THE TRUTH

In 2018, researchers at MIT analyzed 126,000 stories tweeted by more than three million people over eleven years.[64] Their result was stark. False stories were 70 percent more likely to be retweeted than facts and reached people six times faster. The team controlled for bot activity and still found humans were the engine.

Novelty, shock, and outrage moved those stories farther than verification ever could. Platforms designed to maximize engagement rewarded the polarization, giving misinformation a structural advantage.

That pattern helps explain much of what followed. During the first weeks of Russia's full-scale invasion of Ukraine in 2022, video game footage circulated as "real" cockpit views.[65] Years-old explosions were repackaged with fresh captions. Families in basements scrolled their phones trying to decide whether to flee, while recycled images traveled faster than confirmed reporting.

Between 2012 and 2017 in Myanmar, Facebook became a primary channel for anti-Rohingya propaganda.[66] Memes, doctored photos,

---

[64] Soroush Vosoughi, et al., "The spread of true and false news online," *Science*, 359(6380) (2018): 1146–1151, https://doi.org/10.1126/science.aap9559.

[65] Alistair Coleman, "Ukraine conflict: Further false images shared online," *BBC News*, February 25, 2022, https://www.bbc.com/news/60528276.

[66] "Facebook's systems promoted violence against Rohingya; Meta owes reparations," *Amnesty International*, September 29, 2022, https://www.amnesty.org/en/latest/news/2022/09/myanmar-facebooks-systems-promoted-violence-against-rohingya-meta-owes-reparations-new-report/.

and fabricated allegations moved through the platform at a speed local radio could never match. United Nations investigators later concluded that Facebook played a determining role in the violence that followed. The stories did not look sophisticated. They looked familiar and stirred emotions. Repetition did the rest.

During the COVID-19 pandemic, claims about miracle cures, microchips in vaccines, and 5G towers spread with a velocity that outpaced public health guidance.[67] As the virus spread, so did its digital twin. Social media posts raced ahead of public health guidance. Verified voices lent credibility to chaos. Algorithms rewarded outrage, and confusion led the contagion.

While these examples differ in politics and context, they follow the same pattern. Emotionally charged stories travel fastest in systems that reward outrage over accuracy. By the time ethical questions surface, the damage is already in motion.

ADVOCACY, MISINFORMATION, PROPAGANDA

Every story asks us for something, whether it's our attention, belief, or loyalty. Some pieces of content do this with honesty, while others do this to intentionally manipulate. They're all produced for persuasion. The underlying question for us as the creators, storytellers, and consumers we are is, *What's the motivation?*

---

[67] "Managing the COVID-19 infodemic: Promoting healthy behaviours and mitigating the harm from misinformation and disinformation," World Health Organization, September 23, 2020, https://www.who.int/news/item/23-09-2020-managing-the-covid-19-infodemic-promoting-healthy-behaviours-and-mitigating-the-harm-from-misinformation-and-disinformation.

Advocacy: At its best, advocacy uses persuasion to illuminate truth and give language to what has been ignored. It turns private pain into public urgency and connects lived experience to systems that need to change. Done well, it expands empathy and accountability. But advocacy is also influenced by passion, and passion can distort. Even the most principled advocates risk bending facts to fit a narrative that feels morally right. In moments of crisis or conviction, the difference between amplifying truth and editing it can blur. The ethical task is to use story to clarify reality, not overwrite it.

Misinformation moves differently. It spreads quickly, fueled by emotion and the impulse to share information or opinions that feel urgent. Often it doesn't begin with malice, but with carelessness. This may come in the form of a misread headline, a cropped video, or a post shared without pause. Once released, it takes on a life of its own. In an attention economy, accuracy creates friction, and friction slows the feed. The result is a system where falsehood travels faster than fact, not because people are malicious, but because urgency is rewarded over understanding.

Propaganda sits at the far end of the spectrum, using story to create power, while deliberately lacking nuance. It can be coercive or constructive. In its darker form, it disciplines and deceives, rewarding loyalty and punishing dissent. But propaganda is also used to mobilize resistance, promote public health, and expose injustice. What defines its nature is the intent behind it—the deliberate coordination of narrative to direct what people believe and how they behave.

On a screen, all three of these persuasive tactics can take the same form in a polished video with a confident voiceover and a clean emotional arc. The differences are revealed in their function. Advocacy (at its best) discloses its purpose and stands by the facts. Misinformation confuses truth with noise. Propaganda often mixes fact with fiction until the line between them blurs, making the message feel both credible and unquestionable.

For many of us, learning the difference between all of these is an online survival skill, one that determines whether the stories we share cultivate understanding and cooperation or destroy it.

WHO GETS TO TELL THE STORY?

If we're being critical and constructive about the stories fed to us every day, we're asking questions about authorship. Who is being centered? Who's doing the editing? Who's benefiting from this story spreading?

In taking the time to do this we can consider some possible missteps. A nonprofit launches a campaign about food insecurity that never involves families who are navigating the issue. A streaming series dramatizes refugee trauma without handing the mic to migrants themselves. A brand posts an Indigenous land acknowledgment while its supply chain profits from extraction on that same land. The images and words may look righteous, while the practice underneath is to continue with extraction.

Ethical storytelling is rooted in relationship. It begins with invitation and continues with collaboration. People deserve to recognize themselves in the narratives that use their names. They also deserve for these stories to convey more than stereotypes and labels. Dignity includes layers, humor, skill, community, and agency.

When storytellers compress people into symbols, the audience learns shortcuts that may later influence behavior, culture, and policy. We start to hear talking points that insinuate ideas like all protesters are agitators or rioters, all immigrants are criminals, and all conservatives are racist. These blanket stereotypes reduce human lives to easily circulated or dismissed data, becoming the building blocks of narrative inequity—the uneven distribution of whose stories are told, heard, amplified, and protected.

This imbalance is reinforced by the biggest platforms governing how stories spread and gain visibility.

PLATFORM LOGIC AND THE OUTRAGE INCENTIVE

In social feeds wired for inflammation, subtlety sinks, often at the sake of humanity. Even some of the most seasoned journalists and advocates can feel the drag toward spectacle, trimming nuance from their posts just to stay visible.

During the Black Lives Matter uprisings of 2020,[68] clips of broken windows often traveled faster than context about why thousands were in the streets. In several countries, AI-generated images in subsequent conflicts achieved greater reach than verified photographs. In immigration coverage across news cycles, aerial shots of crowded border crossings flattened all nuance into threat. The feed favors the image that can be decoded in one glance, even when that image distorts reality.

[68] "George Floyd protests: Misleading images and videos that have been shared on social media," *BBC Bitesize*, accessed December 15, 2025, https://www.bbc.co.uk/bitesize/articles/zwjqcmn.

None of this is new to you if you spend time online. The question is how to account for these incentives when deciding what tradeoffs come with that choice.

CASE STUDIES IN ONLINE NARRATIVE POWER

1) **Standing Rock and the Live Camera**
   In 2016 at the Standing Rock Sioux Reservation, water protectors opposed the Dakota Access Pipeline through prayer camps, legal motions, and a networked media strategy that turned phones into press passes.[69] Livestreams from the camps showed daily life unfolding in kitchens, schools, elders speaking, drum circles, and winter prep. They also documented police actions in real time. National outlets were slow to arrive. The streams made absence visible and built an archive that outlived the news cycle. That archive still helps communities teach the next generation how mobilization looks when extraction meets resolve.
2) **WhatsApp Rumors and Mob Violence in India**
   In parts of India, rumors about child kidnappers spread through encrypted WhatsApp groups over several years.[70] Old or unrelated videos were repeatedly recirculated with local place names and urgent warnings. Because the messages came from friends, family, and neighbors, they were imbued with an air of trust.

---

[69] Meiling Colorado, "Standing Rock became not just a simple protest, but a working, living example of what was possible, what could be done," *Permaculture Women's Guild*, accessed January 14, 2026, https://www.permaculturewomen.com/standing-rock/.

[70] "India lynchings: WhatsApp sets new rules after mob killings," *BBC*, July 20, 2018, https://www.bbc.com/news/world-asia-india-44897714.

In multiple towns, these rumors sparked mob violence, and innocent people were attacked. WhatsApp's design and easy function of forwarding within private groups allowed misinformation to travel faster than corrections. Governments responded with arrests and pressure on the platform to limit forwarding, while communities launched media literacy campaigns and public announcements to counter the rumors.

The case shows how private networks can function as mass broadcast systems and how remediation requires both platform changes and local culture work.

3) **Climate Delay Tactics**

For decades, some industry-funded campaigns refined a strategy of delay rather than outright denial, regarding climate change. As scientific consensus around human-caused climate change hardened, the message shifted from *"climate change isn't real"* to *"solutions are too expensive," "technology will save us later,"* or *"individual behavior matters more than policy."* Oil and gas trade groups funded messaging that emphasized uncertainty, economic anxiety, or personal responsibility, while avoiding structural change. These narratives sound reasonable in isolation and devastating in aggregate. They convert urgency into postponement, offering reassurance without accountability. Naming delay as a narrative pattern helps audiences recognize it when it arrives dressed as pragmatism.

THE SLOW WORK THAT OUTLASTS A FEED

Fast stories spike attention. But it's often slow stories that foster understanding. When you think back to a piece of content that stayed with you, was it a post that trended for a day or an essay you went back to read? Was it a podcast that introduced you to a voice you hadn't heard before or a long investigation that traced decisions, money, and consequences until a pattern became clear?

Slow storytelling channels voltage because it's generous with context and precise with claims. The subject reviews the quotes. The call to action is specific and within reach. And the audience is trusted to sit with depth.

BRAND AND MEDIA HYPOCRISY

Ethical breakdowns in media happen regularly, often in ways that go unnoticed. A company posts about racial justice while maintaining a leadership team that reflects none of the communities in its ads. A story may reduce migration to data points, then seamlessly shift to lifestyle coverage. The proximity undermines both topics, turning human movement and leisure into interchangeable content.

An influencer may use another person's trauma as the foundation for a carousel of inspirational takeaways and product links. These choices teach the audience to treat people as material, and repetition normalizes it.

Repairing this kind of construct can unfold through unglamorous choices made over time by who gets hired, who gets paid, whose expertise is trusted, and whose work is credited. It happens in editorial meetings, in sourcing decisions, and in whether corrections are published and conflicts are disclosed. Integrity accumulates through practice.

A FIELD GUIDE FOR ETHICAL STORYTELLING

If you're creating content or simply consuming it, here's a set of practices you can reach for when a deadline looms or the feed is loud.

Truth as Baseline. Source your claims. Check dates, locations, and provenance before you share a clip. If you cannot verify, withhold. If you publish and later learn you were wrong, correct with the same energy you used to share.

Context as Kindness. Add at least a paragraph that explains what came before the event. Identify the system, not only the symptom. Link to longer reporting. Help your audience discover what you found.

Consent as Relationship. If you are using someone else's story, involve them. Explain how it will be used, where it will live, and when it will end. Give them the chance to decline. Build in time for review when safety allows.

Dignity as Frame. Show people as more than pain. Include competence, culture, community, and joy. Trauma-only lenses attract clicks and repel respect.

Transparency as Trust. Disclose your role, funding, partners, and point of view. Say what you know and where the edges are. Ambiguity about motive invites suspicion; clarity builds credibility.

Safety as Threshold. If your story could put someone at risk, remove identifying details or hold publication until protections are in place. If you cannot protect them, do not publish.

Impact-Focused Clarity. Avoid disaster terms for people. Avoid absolutes. If a number is an estimate, say so. If a photo is from a different year, label it.

Design for Slowness. Build friction into your own process: a fact sheet, a buddy edit, a pause before "post." Friction feels costly in the moment and saves reputations later.

FRAMING AND METAPHOR

Frames are shortcuts the brain uses to assign meaning. They are efficient and sticky, which makes them dangerous in the wrong hands. When immigration is framed as a "surge," the mind looks for levees. When the opioid crisis is framed as a "war," budgets shift toward enforcement and weaponry instead of treatment and prevention. When a neighborhood is framed as a "no-go zone," the map erases the people who live and work there.

Choose frames that illuminate systems and people rather than panic. If you need a metaphor, reach for ones that invite stewardship and responsibility.

- Climate as home maintenance.
- Democracy as muscle.
- Public health as neighborliness.

These frames carry action without contempt. They may be harder to meme, but they last longer.

VISUAL EVIDENCE AND VERIFICATION

Images travel farther than paragraphs. Think of them as testimonies. When you can, inspect their EXIF data (metadata) when you can.

Run a reverse-image search. Compare shadows to the local time of day. And read signage and license plates. Ask whether an image depicts the event being claimed or whether it was lifted from another moment and repackaged with a fresh caption. If your audience shares a miscaptioned image because you rushed, your credibility pays the bill.

When you publish a video, label edits. If safety requires a blur or a cut, explain that choice in a line under the player. If you received a clip from an activist group, disclose that relationship. If a translation appears on screen, link to the transcript and name the translator. Visual honesty may attract fewer clicks, but it builds credibility, which will serve you and the story in the long run.

TEMPLATES FOR DISCLOSURE

Create boilerplate language for the disclosures you face most often. They might be funding relationships, production partnerships, corrections, anonymization methods, and conflicts of interest. Keep the language plain. Publish the template once so you can point to it later. When you decline a story because consent was not granted or safety could not be secured, say so. The public learns ethics by watching you practice.

TRAINING AND CULTURE

Ethical storytelling is easier inside teams that treat it as routine. Run tabletop exercises where a rumor hits your desks on a Friday night and the pressure is to post by the hour. Assign roles, practice the pause, and rehearse the correction. Keep a shared document of decisions you admire from other outlets and creators. Culture is a library of lived choices.

THE STORYTELLING COMPASS

Before you publish, ask:

1. Whose story is this?
2. What is my intention?
3. What is missing?
4. Who could this harm? Who could it help?
5. What would I want if this were about me?

View these five questions as a brake, not a wall. They can help slow you down long enough to make a wiser decision.

BREAKING THE BUBBLE

It goes without saying that polarization thickens inside sealed rooms. Feeds filled with agreement can feel safe and affirming to the point that any unfamiliar perspectives begin to feel completely distorted. Over time, repetition narrows the field of vision.

Some people counter this by widening their inputs. This includes reading across outlets, following voices far from their own experience, noticing which accounts reward outrage and which reward understanding. Others step away from screens altogether, turning to in-person spaces where disagreement carries texture and consequence like a town hall or a clinic waiting room. Real-life proximity typically has a stronger chance of restoring humanity.

EXERCISES FOR PRACTICE

The following drills are designed for you, your team, or your classroom. You can use them to evolve ethics from concept into muscle.

1) **The Origin Check**
   Pick one viral clip. As a group, trace its origin. When was it first posted? Where? By whom? What changed as it crossed platforms? Write a short brief that documents the path and the distortions. Discuss how you would caption it if you had to share it responsibly or whether you would share it at all.
2) **The Consent Map**
   For a story you are currently telling, list every person who appears, speaks, or is referenced. Mark who has granted consent, who needs context, and who requires safety measures. Decide what changes you will make to honor those needs. Update your production plan accordingly.
3) **Language Audit**
   Pull ten recent headlines or captions you have written. Circle metaphors and labels. Replace disaster-coded phrases with accurate descriptions. Replace passive voice with active voice where responsibility matters. Share your edits with a peer and invite theirs.
4) **The Stakeholder Table**
   Draw a table with four columns: directly affected, adjacent, decision-makers, and distant audience. For a single story, list stakeholders in each column. Next to each, note what they need to know, what could harm them, and how they might participate in the telling. Adjust your story structure to reflect that map.

5) **The Slow Story Sprint**
   Give yourself forty-eight hours to report and publish a mini-feature that still meets the standards above. The time constraint simulates news pressure, while the checklist keeps you from cutting ethical corners. Debrief what worked and what didn't.
6) **The Correction Drill**
   Write a hypothetical correction for a story you liked that later required changes. Model tone, specificity, and repair steps. Get comfortable with the language of accountability so you do not freeze when it is your turn.

YOUR MIC CHECK

Before you pick up the mic or hit publish, run a quick diagnostic:

- What does this story do to the people inside it?
- Where did this claim come from, and have I verified the source?
- Am I compressing a person into a symbol?
- Would I stand by this in a room with the people I'm describing?

This check takes two minutes and saves months of damage control. It also shifts your attention from performance to consequence, which is where ethical judgement begins.

TURN UP THE VOLUME

After the check, choose where to direct your volume. You can take this opportunity to elevate voices that rarely clear the algorithm.

Perhaps you'd like to share work by local reporters who have been covering an issue for years or link to organizers who hold the context you lack.

Pair emotion with instructions that may include phone numbers, budget hearings, comment periods, and meeting dates. When you critique, offer a path. When you praise, share credit.

Volume is not only reach. Volume is repetition. It's your right to repeat accurate frames until they stick, to repeat names and histories that have been erased, and to repeat the distinction between verified and unverified, using language your audience can reuse.

THE DROP

As we've covered in this book so far, stories influence how people understand the world and their place within it. Based on that alone, ethical storytelling is something to revere and practice in repeatable choices.

Ethics shows up in how decisions are made, including what gets framed, what gets left out, whose voice is centered, and whose is treated as expendable. It lives in editorial judgment, in attribution, and in whether nuance is preserved or simplified for reach.

Attention comes with consequences. And we are by all means living in an attention economy. What gains traction influences what feels legitimate, urgent, or worthy of sharing. In environments that reward speed and reaction, restraint becomes a choice.

The work, then, is not louder storytelling. It's more deliberate storytelling. It's choosing accuracy over acceleration, context over reaction, and responsibility over likes. This is how narratives endure beyond the moment they circulate—beyond the mic drop.

10

WITNESSING THE EDGES: AT THE BORDERS OF CONFLICT AND RESILIENCE

In every story of survival, there is a hero. Sometimes, that hero is simply you refusing to give up.

—Elizabeth Gilbert

Standing in the middle of a dirt road at the border of Syria and Jordan, I stared into a horizon that to my eyes looked initially like a kind of purgatory, an expanse of muted tents and caravans stretching across the barren desert. The Syrian civil war[71] raged just miles away as dust swirled around the World Food Programme vehicle escorting

[71] "Syria profile—Timeline," *BBC News*, January 14, 2019, https://www.bbc.com/news/world-middle-east-14703995.

me to Za'atari, the world's largest camp for Syrian refugees, home to nearly 150,000 people.[72]

Crossing the entrance gate, alternating waves of intrigue and sadness hit me. Rows of prefabricated shelters spread across the two-mile-wide settlement, their uniformity broken only by tarps rippling in the wind. But the closer we moved toward the center, the more I began to notice life pulsing beneath its surface.

The desert air carried a dry, metallic tang that clung to the back of my throat. The silence was heavy, punctuated by the low hum of diesel generators and the occasional crackle of a loudspeaker announcing aid distributions.

Then, just as quickly, the soundscape shifted.

Children's laughter cut through the stillness as they chased a ball across the road, their mother calling them back toward home. A cart squealed as its wheels hit uneven ground. And then I saw the market street, which revealed another face of Za'atari altogether. Stalls constructed from corrugated metal and wood lined the thoroughfare, painted in bursts of color that pushed back against the monotony of white caravans. Vendors sold everything from falafel to SIM cards to wedding dresses. Strings of secondhand shoes dangled like trophies. A tailor hunched over a sewing machine while a teenager scrolled on his phone nearby.

Still, there were moments when the weight of my intrusion pressed in.

---

[72] "Za'atari Camp Factsheet," *United Nations High Commissioner for Refugees*, December 2024, https://reliefweb.int/attachments/ea753d3e-b643-484a-a033-40c6fb5144cc/Zaatari%20Fact%20Sheet_December%202024.pdf.

There weren't many people walking the streets, but the few I did see wore a look of resignation in their eyes that I imagine only the feelings that come with displacement can etch in a person's soul. My first twenty minutes felt like I was barging in on a conversation not meant for me, the kind where silence shouts, *Get out.*

"Maybe I shouldn't be here," I muttered under my breath.

"You're fine," my guide reassured me. "People here are used to seeing visitors from all over the world. Just be sure to ask permission before you take photos. Come. I'll take you to see how the tech works."

Ah, the tech. That was why I had come.

I had arrived looking for a story about technology because I'd heard about a supermarket that ran on blockchain. After years of reading white papers and listening to promises about innovation solving everything from hunger to inequality, I wanted to see what those claims looked like when translated into real life.

We walked toward Tazweed, one of the camp's two grocery stores. Inside, a cashier demonstrated how the system worked. Shoppers verified their identity through an iris scan, which accessed a World Food Programme-managed account to settle the bill. No cash or cards were required. The technology reduced fraud, lowered transaction costs, and returned a measure of choice to people whose options had long been constrained.

I left the store less impressed by the technology than by the intention behind it.

Za'atari wasn't only a site of displacement. It was a place where continuity persisted and where dignity was practiced daily.

Image 9. Customers and a cashier using the blockchain system at Tazweed grocery store in Za'atari. January 2019.

THE THREADS OF THE TAPESTRY

After visiting the grocery store, my guide took me to the settlement's Oasis Center for Resilience and Empowerment of Women and Girls, a UN Women-run program established in 2012. It offers a safe space where participants can access emergency aid, specialized gender-based violence services, and educational and creative programs for women and their children.[73] Inside, the kids were playing in the childcare facility while their mothers were assembling crafts. The women invited me to sit down at the table where they were making jewelry.

Due to privacy concerns, I'm not revealing too much about individual refugees. But I am sharing some stories that have already been published online.

Tamara possessed skills in painting, embroidery, and crafts before being displaced by the Syrian war. However, she lacked a platform to utilize these talents for economic gain. At the Made in Za'atari Center,[74] Tamara found an opportunity to generate income for her family by creating and selling handmade accessories. The center provided her with the necessary resources and a marketplace to sell her products. Tamara's initiative not only supports her family financially but also showcases the potential of leveraging traditional crafts for economic empowerment among refugee women.

Before the Syrian conflict, Ena'am[75] was illiterate and had always dreamed of becoming a cosmetologist. After arriving at Za'atari, she committed herself to learning the basics of reading and writing, which enabled her to enroll in a comprehensive cosmetology training program conducted by Blumont at the Made in Za'atari Center. She now runs the beauty salon there, trains other women from the camp in hairdressing and cosmetics, and earns an income to support her family.

There are many more stories like this of refugees running classrooms, cutting hair in barber shops, and making music in Za'atari.

---

[73] "Empowerment through employment for Syrian refugee women in Jordan," *UN Women News*, August 10, 2018, https://www.unwomen.org/en/news/stories/2018/8/feature-empowerment-through-employment-for-syrian-refugee-women-in-jordan.

[74] "Made in Za'atari: Women Refugee Entrepreneurs Make Their Mark," Blumont International, October 23, 2023, https://blumont.org/project/made-in-zaatari/.

[75] Blumont, "Made in Za'atari."

Before I left, the women sang to me and gave me three pieces of jewelry. What started as a scene of despondence and despair ended up as a collection of stories about people not letting their situation strip them of their human dignity, creativity, or ingenuity, but rather cultivating these qualities further.

What struck me most as I left wasn't only their generosity, but how completely it contradicted the dominant narrative told about refugees in many parts of the world. The people I met were artists, teachers, entrepreneurs, and musicians—people who had built lives, nurtured ambitions, and cultivated expertise long before war forced them across a border. Those details rarely survive the journey into a headline. Somewhere between displacement and coverage, entire lives are compressed into a single label, and individuality is traded for abstraction. The distance between who people are and how they are portrayed is often where fear takes hold.

The word "refugees" itself is steeped in stigmas, rooted less in reality than in misunderstanding or misrepresentation.[76] When I was living between London and Paris during the Syrian War, refugees were often painted as burdens on resources, potential threats to security, competitors for jobs or housing, disruptors of cultural norms. Today, stereotypes continue to linger around poverty and helplessness, obscuring resilience and contribution. Some accuse all refugees of exploiting asylum systems or falsely claiming danger to seek opportunity. And then there is the most insidious assumption—that displacement is permanent, that refugees will never return, never integrate, and never belong.

---

[76] Alexander Betts and Paul Collier, *Refuge: Transforming a broken refugee system* (Penguin Books, 2017).

Claudia Kozman, et al., "The Role of Media and Communication in Reducing Uncertainty During the Syria War," *Media and Communication* 9, no. 4 (2021): 297–308, https://doi.org/10.17645/mac.v9i4.4352.

What Za'atari showed me was the opposite. Across the caravans, plenty of individuals were making the most of their situation. Many of the people I saw were not waiting passively for the world to change their conditions. They were living their lives with the resources and dignity they had. They were defying the mainstream narrative with their individual and collective power to create.

Image 10. Women teaching their kids at the Oasis Center for Resilience and Empowerment of Women and Girls in Za'atari. January 2019.

Image 11. A main street in the Za'atari refugee camp, on the border of Syria and Jordan. January 2019.

Image 12. Storefronts, businesses, and vendors in Za'atari. January 2019.

YOUR MIC CHECK

Headlines are designed for speed. They simplify, condense, and move on. And more often than not, important parts of a story go missing, not because no one knows them, but because they're harder to hold in a tight frame. For many of us, seeing or hearing headlines from a news outlet or an internet personality is how we learn about the world beyond our immediate reach. But we can usually feel when a story is being flattened.

This mic check is an invitation to trust that instinct. You don't need to fill in every gap you come across in the news or start commenting about wars on Instagram. What you can do that won't cost you anything more than a few extra minutes of your time is give yourself permission to linger a little longer with the stories that pass in front of you each day.

Sometimes that means noticing what a headline makes legible right away. Other times, it means realizing there's more beneath the surface than what fits into a few lines. You don't need expertise or insider knowledge to recognize that there's more to a story than what's being revealed.

Over time, paying attention this way builds confidence. You start to see how stories are assembled, how certain angles rise to the top, and how others remain just outside the frame. That awareness gives you more freedom in what you share, what you repeat, and how you relate to the world around you.

TURN UP THE VOLUME

Here are practices you can use to expand any headline into a fuller, more human narrative:

- **Peel Back the Layers.** Ask: *Who else is affected?* If a company merges, how does it impact cafeteria workers or small vendors? If a war dominates the front page, what does it mean for a child trying to finish homework in a camp?
- **Walk a Mile.** Choose someone outside the spotlight and imagine their day. Where are they, what are they feeling, what obstacles shape them?
- **Flip the Frame.** Tell the story from a different vantage point. Not the policymaker, but the grassroots organizer. Not the CEO, but the person on the factory floor.
- **Interview the Story.** Even in your mind, ask: *What was life like before this? What do you wish people knew? How has this changed you?*
- **Map the Web.** Draw connections from decision-makers to the people they'll never meet, but whose lives they still impact.
- **Challenge What's Missing.** Whose voice is loudest here? Whose silence is most deafening?
- **Reframe the Headline.** Rewrite it to center people. "Floods Devastate Region" becomes "A Mother Rebuilds After the Flood."
- **Imagine the Diary.** Write a journal entry from someone inside the story, not as performance, but as practice in empathy.

Each of these tools is a way of refusing one dimensionality. They remind us that behind every policy or crisis are human beings with names and dreams.

THE DROP

An infinite number of stories are far more human than what's typically handed to us. They're discovered when we look closer, travel and listen deeper, and refuse to accept what we see and hear online and on-air as the full story.

When we practice peeling back layers and flipping frames, we sharpen our empathy and align more with the universal truth that we're all more alike than we are different.

We dismantle the systems that thrive on treating people as symbols instead of whole lives.

Your invitation as the bold, brilliant, and bodacious storyteller that you are, whether in a newsroom, on a stage, in a classroom, or at your own dinner table, is to keep asking: *Who else is impacted? What truth lies beyond the surface?*

When you commit to telling stories that stretch beyond headlines, you're not simply amplifying voices. You're shifting narratives. And that shift breaks down invisible borders in our hearts and minds.

PART 4

MODULATING UP

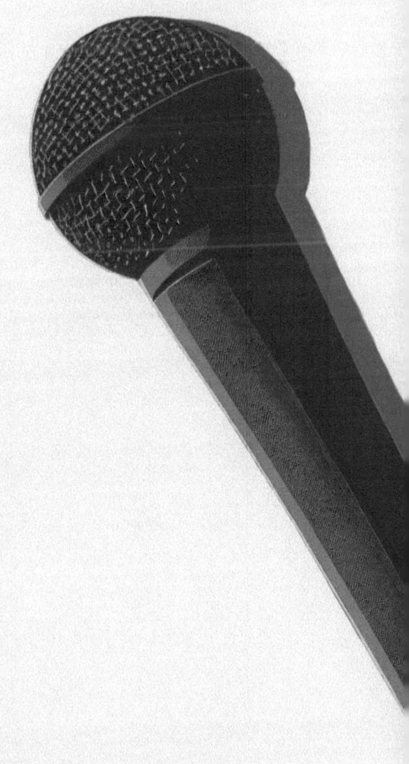

11

PLOTTING PEACE: CONFLICT, COEXISTENCE, AND CREATION

Stories can conquer fear, you know. They can make the heart bigger.

—Ben Okri

On a crisp afternoon in 2018, I drove into the Judean mountains with a few new friends from Ramallah. The road wound through sun-bleached hills into olive groves and stone terraces. The terrain was rugged and alive.

We were heading to Rawabi,[77] a new Palestinian city still under construction north of Ramallah. In the front seat, Omar, my personal guide, pointed as we drove to towers rising from dust. I met him through Tech2Peace, where Israeli and Palestinian youth learn

[77] Rawabi official website, accessed November 22, 2025, https://rawabi.ps/.

technology and engage in conflict resolution.[78] Watching him map possibilities onto the landscape felt like an extension of that work.

His hand traced the horizon, then settled on a carved slope in the distance. A stone amphitheater had already been cut into it, precise and improbable. He said it would hold 20,000 people. For a moment, the city felt finished.

When we arrived at the top of the mountain, our guides called the area the Palestinian Silicon Valley, as it was designed to spark a tech economy and a new sense of home. What I took away from hearing this was that Rawabi was a declaration that "home" could be built from both history and imagination. Cranes were suspended over half-constructed buildings and roads led to places yet to exist. Years later, much of it remains incomplete.

And yet, even in its partial form, Rawabi evoked something rare, a vision under construction. For many Palestinians, it stood for what it means to insist on belonging, even when the world denies you completion. My guides spoke of it with the pride and affection of people describing both a place and a promise. For them, building this destination was an act of persistence.

Looking out across the terraces and stone foundations, I reflected on an idea I'd been traveling with for years: that belonging doesn't always mean being settled. Sometimes it means building while the ground beneath you is still shifting.

[78] Tech2Peace, accessed November 22, 2025, https://www.tech2peace.com/.

Image 13. My guides in the amphitheater of Rawabi, the first urban planned city built for Palestinians by Palestinians. January 2018.

* * *

After touring Rawabi, I spent the next few days meeting with Palestinian entrepreneurs across the West Bank. They were bright and hungry, building communications platforms and startups that delivered everything from fashion apparel to security software and hardware. I marveled at the creativity and drive of an entrepreneurial community in a place that seemed designed to keep people's ideas small.

They told me about funding gaps, slow internet, and all the daily nuisances. But nearly all of their stories circled back to the same principle of hope, along with the same obstacle of blockades to freedom of movement for people, goods and services, and any normal flow of business.

They described how checkpoints could appear overnight, how a route that took twenty minutes on Tuesday might take two hours on Thursday, and how a contract might vanish because they couldn't show up on time.

Little did I know then that just days later, I'd be walking through the most infamous military checkpoint of all—Qalandia—a place known at the time for its demoralizing waits, flashes of violence nearby, and the feeling of being herded like livestock through metal turnstiles.

My last night in the West Bank, I went out dancing in Ramallah with Omar and some of the startup founders I met that day. Every song and dance served up a full-blown celebration. Each tune came from a different corner of the Middle East. Arabic pop, Turkish beats, and Egyptian love songs serenaded us, as we danced like we'd been waiting all year for that moment. Joy rippled through the crowd, and for a few hours the checkpoints, the headlines, the maps with their sharp dividing lines all dissolved.

QALANDA, COEXISTENCE, AND THE BELLS OF JERUSALEM

The next morning, I was spent. I could barely lift my head. But I was determined to see Jerusalem before heading back to Tel Aviv. I packed my bag and ran to the hotel entrance to say goodbye to Omar, who was flagging down a taxi for me.

"Keep building and moving," he said. "And keep dancing. We have to keep dancing through all of this, you know."

His words and the tender look in his eyes softened the tension in my forehead, and for a glorious second my hangover subsided.

A few miles into a bumpy ride, I started cursing myself as my head pounded louder and louder. Then, my driver suddenly came to an abrupt stop. He had pulled over at the entrance to Qalandia.

"Oh!" I said. "You're not driving me through?"

He shook his head. "I can't. Not with a Palestinian license plate."

Days earlier, I'd read about the Qalandia checkpoint.[79] To prepare for the trip, I had watched videos that showed grainy footage of packed lines and people pressed shoulder to shoulder under flickering fluorescent lights. I'd heard the stories from journalists and fixers alike about the hours-long waits, the unpredictable closures, the way the air itself seemed to thicken with tension and exhaustion.

I stepped out of the car, still wearing my pastel pink coat and carrying my purple suitcase, painfully aware that I looked like the ultimate American tourist. Once I got to the line, time moved like a sloth. The queue crawled between metal barricades built less for guidance than control. It felt like we were being funneled through a cattle chute with every move dictated by unseen hands.

No one talked. The man ahead of me kept checking his watch. A woman balanced a squirming toddler on her hip. An older man leaned on the railing, eyes hollow, like he'd stood there a thousand times.

Finally, when the turnstile buzzed three hours later, I handed over the papers I'd collected at the airport, unsure of which one was the correct slip. Two young Israeli soldiers passed the papers back, advising me to find another one. I gave them a stray small note I found in my pocket that looked kind of like it had a stamp on it. They reviewed it quickly and motioned for me to walk through.

---

[79] United Nations Office for the Coordination of Humanitarian Affairs (OCHA) in the Occupied Palestinian Territory, accessed November 22, 2025, https://www.ochaopt.org.

On the other side, I found my guide Rana waiting. A young woman with bright, steady, and watchful eyes and a calm that felt both meditative and edged, she was a graduate of Tech2Peace. She had offered to show me around Old City Jerusalem before I drove back to Tel Aviv. In four hours she gave me the greatest history lesson I've ever experienced. She led me through narrow alleyways that seemed like secret passages. She guided me to worn stones, telling stories about every corner and numerous families that had been pushed out, disappeared, or come back to now live in coexistence.

As she spoke, what stayed with me wasn't the grandeur of domes or ancient walls, but the sound around us. Bells rang from churches. The call to prayer spiraled from nearby mosques. Voices spilled from market stalls. Jerusalem doesn't keep time with a single bell. Each quarter—Jewish, Muslim, Christian, Armenian—moves to its own rhythm. The city hums in overlapping cadences, discordant and miraculous in their persistence.

At the top of a tower by the Church of the Redeemer, we stood listening. Rana told me she didn't hope for peace the way most people meant it.

"I hope for space," she said. "I hope people stop shouting long enough to realize they're standing on shared ground."

That word "space" stayed with me. What it made me feel is that Jerusalem is held together by practice—by people holding space, conflict, and identity, and still choosing daily coexistence. That's what a story does when it's allowed to breathe. It names the scars, and sometimes the naming alone helps us heal. It doesn't insist we're all the same. It invites us to stay, side by side, listening, even when we've been programmed to close ourselves.

Jerusalem doesn't offer space or peace through resolution. It offers them through a negotiated and imperfect choreography.

People there choose to remain, to walk the same streets, share the same skyline, and let their stories collide.

If we ever want to plot peace in the Middle East, in the United States, or anywhere lines are drawn too deep, we can start by telling our stories fully, and then making room for someone else to stand beside them.

This is where narrative becomes more than just a tool and a form of coexistence—not the kind that asks us to dilute our histories or blur our beliefs, but the kind that says, "I'll keep speaking my story. And I'll make room for yours, too."

Standing there with Rana, I thought about how much of a conflict comes down to who gets to narrate reality. In Jerusalem, everyone's telling their own version of what the land is, what it means, and who belongs to it. But instead of harmonizing, they overlap. And in that overlap, there's dissonance, but there's also presence.

That's the kind of storytelling I believe in, the kind that doesn't resolve tension but acknowledges it. The kind that doesn't demand uniformity but invites understanding. The kind that doesn't require you to silence yourself to listen, and instead asks you to listen as deeply as you speak.

Rana told me how Tech2Peace had taught her to hold more than one truth at a time. Growing up, she'd heard one version of the conflict. At the workshops, she heard another. Neither experience erased the other, but having both carved out more space for understanding each of them.

I imagine that at first, to stretch like this may feel like you're betraying your loved ones and even a part of yourself. But eventually, if you stay in the discomfort long enough, your understanding begins to expand like a muscle lengthening into a new range of motion.

That's what storytelling can do. It can create space for the people around us to be more whole by expanding the boundaries of what we think we're allowed to believe.

By the end of our walk, the city was starting to dim. The gold of late afternoon had turned silver. I could hear the low rumble of street vendors closing up. In the distance, another bell rang. This one was slow and deliberate, signaling a transition by its tone.

In my limited time in Jerusalem, the city showed me that some of the most complex and nuanced people and places have no clear answer. But they stay together by practice, restraint, patience, and memory—side by side.

Image 14. Old City Jerusalem. January 2018.

Image 15. Burning a wish in Old City Jerusalem. January 2018.

STORIES CAN CHANGE. AND WHEN THEY DO, THEY CHANGE US

Cognitive neuroscientist Dr. Emile Bruneau spent his career studying how storytelling affects intergroup dynamics.[80] His research

[80] Emile G. Bruneau and Rebecca Saxe, "The power of being heard: The benefits of 'perspective-giving' in the context of intergroup conflict," *Journal of Experimental Social Psychology*, 48, no. 4 (2012): 855–866, https://doi.org/10.1016/j.jesp.2012.02.017.

showed that when individuals hear personal, emotionally resonant stories from someone on the "opposite side" of a conflict, their brains respond with increased empathy and decreased bias.

This phenomenon, called narrative transportation, allows listeners to become immersed in another person's experience, suspending judgment and creating space for connection. Bruneau's work, along with that of researchers like Dr. Uri Hasson at Princeton, suggests that storytelling isn't just metaphorically transformative. It's neurologically transformative.[81] When we share our stories, our brains begin to align. We quite literally get on the same wavelength.

This is the power behind Tech2Peace. Their dialogue sessions are grounded in neuroscience, structured around trust-building, and intentionally designed to lower the psychological defenses that conflict erects. The young people in Tech2Peace's program aren't just learning to code; they're unlearning fear. They're not pretending the political situation isn't dire. They're fully aware of the risks, but they're choosing, against all odds, to build something together anyway.

The night my Israeli peace activist friends brought me to Ramallah made that clear. No one in the room showed any trace of ignorance or ego. No one claimed to have the answers. What they offered was presence. They had shown up, again and again, across borders to engage in the slow, dedicated work of storytelling for conflict resolution.

Some of the issues they addressed weren't by any means unique to the Middle East. Some echoes were painfully familiar. In the United States, our divisions may not appear in the form of

---

[81] Uri Hasson, et al., "Brain-to-brain coupling: A mechanism for creating and sharing a social world," *Trends in Cognitive Sciences*, 16, no. 2 (2012): 114–121, https://doi.org/10.1016/j.tics.2011.12.007.

checkpoints or permits, but they are just as real. We've replaced dialogue with verbally destroying one another behind online profiles and wide-eyed curiosity with fist-clenching defensiveness. We exist inside ideological bubbles and echo chambers that reward certainty and punish nuance. Our walls are digital, but they're fortified just the same.

Even though my visit to Israel and Palestine was pre-Gaza War, I still meditate on the lessons I took home with me. Those walls are not permanent. In fact, like conflict narratives themselves, they are maintained by repetition, which means they can begin to be deprogrammed and disrupted by something as simple as a story.

And right now, America is a country starved for deprogramming.

We are a nation in the midst of a narrative crisis. Our collective imagination has been hijacked by outrage cycles and political theater. We're no longer just arguing about what's true. We're fighting over whose pain is real, whose perspectives deserve airtime, and whose version of America gets to define the rest of us. We don't just disagree. We dehumanize.

Ask someone what it means to be "American" today, and you'll get a different story depending on who you ask and which news outlet or podcast they watch. Is it rugged individualism or collective responsibility? Is it a beacon of democracy or a crumbling empire? Is it a nation built on freedom or one haunted by the ghosts of unacknowledged harm?

The truth is, all of those stories are in circulation at once. And when there's no shared moral compass or narrative, the country becomes a cacophony.

Much like in conflict zones abroad, the United States is seeing a rise in identity-based storytelling that trades empathy for absolutes. Political affiliation has become a proxy for moral character.

Disagreement is mistaken for betrayal. On both the right and the left, we're regularly encouraged to see "the other side" not just as wrong, but as dangerous.

And yet, beneath that polarization there's still a pulse and a persistent desire to be understood. That's where storytelling comes in, creating space for us to say, "Here's who I am. Here's what I fear. Here's where I hurt."

In a deeply divided nation, storytelling offers a way to move beyond performative solidarity or intellectual abstraction. It roots us in embodied reality. It's what allows a rancher in Texas and a public school teacher in Chicago to find common ground, possibly in pain, pride, or dreams for the next generation.

Across the country, small-scale storytelling projects are already doing this work. StoryCorps records and preserves everyday people's life stories to build connection and understanding. Narrative 4 brings people together in guided story exchanges that help participants listen deeply and recognize one another's humanity. The People's Supper organizes shared dinners where participants across ideological and cultural divides are invited to talk and build trust.[82] The results aren't always neat or uplifting, but they are real. And realness, in an age of algorithmic outrage, can be transformative.

I think about my time in the West Bank often when I see Americans bravely attempting to speak across differences. I think about the older Palestinian men who weren't sure peace would come in their lifetimes, and the younger ones who believed it still might. I think about how no one in the room demanded consensus.

---

[82] StoryCorps, accessed November 22, 2025, https://storycorps.org/about/. Narrative 4, accessed November 22, 2025, https://narrative4.com/about-n4/. The People's Supper, accessed November 22, 2025, https://thepeoplessupper.org/.

What they asked for instead was space to be heard, to be complex, and to not have to perform their pain in a way that fit someone else's framework.

That's the kind of space we need more of here in the United States.

We need more people who are willing to say, "Tell me the story behind your stance," and fewer people broadcasting their own opinions before anyone else has spoken.

It's possible for us to rebuild our capacity to hold contradiction, to recognize that two things can be true at once: that someone's fear can be real, and so can someone else's joy; that systemic injustice exists, and so does individual and collective effort; that the past shapes us, but the future is still ours to create.

One of the most dangerous myths in America today is that unity means uniformity. It doesn't. Unity means that even when we don't agree on how to fix the problem, we're still willing to sit at the same table and say, "Let's figure it out together." It means recognizing that someone's worldview isn't a threat to yours. It's an opportunity to expand the aperture through which you see.

When we lose the ability to hear each other's stories, we lose the ability to imagine a future together. We start fighting to protect the past instead. And that's how nations stall. That's how they fracture. That's how they forget who they are.

But when we make space for stories that don't sound like our own and when we build rooms big enough to stand in with people we were taught to distrust, we start creating a future that's vast enough for all of us.

It doesn't start with grand speeches. It starts in living rooms and union halls, in classrooms and community centers. It starts in the uncomfortable moment when someone says something that challenges you and you don't shut them down. Instead you ask why.

You ask how. You ask what they've lived that made them believe the thing you're curious enough to want to understand.

We may not be able to undo centuries of injustice or rewire entire political systems overnight. But we can decide how we show up in the conversations we're in now. And if enough of us do that—if enough of us take the risk to be vulnerable, to be open, to be kind when it's hardest—we'll begin to build something much harder to destroy than consensus. We'll build human connection.

We'll build muscle memory for democracy.

We'll build resilience for the long fight ahead.

We'll build the kind of country where conflict doesn't signal collapse, but evolution.

Storytelling, at its best, doesn't just help us understand one another. It allows us to become someone new in the process.

So when the noise gets loud, and the lines feel sharp, and the story of America seems like it's tearing in half, remember this. Every nation has a narrative. Every generation gets to edit the next chapter. And every one of us is holding a pen.

What will you write next?

* * *

THE FINAL WORD: THE STORY THAT STARTS WITH US

Peace doesn't descend from treaties or national announcements. It begins in overlooked moments like someone keeping the office open late for strangers, or a car full of people who shouldn't be in the same car, laughing their way into forbidden territory, or a circle of unlikely allies choosing to speak, to listen, and to risk having hope.

While those moments don't solve anything on their own, they make space for something else to begin. They lay the groundwork for renewal. As the late playwright Jonathan Larson once wrote, "The opposite of war isn't peace. It's creation."[83]

The people I met on that journey in Ramallah definitely didn't agree on everything. A few of them didn't even agree on what year the conflict actually started. But they didn't need to. What they shared was a willingness to co-create a story big enough to hold all of their identities, pains, fears, and hopes with dignity—a story that didn't ignore history, but insisted it could still have a sequel.

That's what storytelling makes possible. It reminds us that we are not just the product of the stories we've inherited. We are the authors of the stories still to come.

So the next time you find yourself in conflict, remember that there's no need to defend who you've been. You are allowed to ask yourself who you want to become.

And you can even write that story with someone you were never supposed to trust.

A STORYTELLING PRACTICE FOR A DIVIDED WORLD: THE "THRESHOLD QUESTION"

When we find ourselves in conflict, whether it's across cultures, in politics, or at a barbecue, it's tempting to reach for facts, arguments, or rehearsed beliefs. Not only is there nothing wrong with doing that, sometimes certain scenarios call for us to do that.

[83] Jonathan Larson, "La Vie Bohème," *Rent*, 1996.

But if we want to experience transformation inside or outside of ourselves, it doesn't start with certainty. It begins with curiosity.

Try this: instead of asking "How can I convince them?" ask yourself: "What is the question this person lives at the edge of, and can I meet them there?"

This is the Threshold Question—the unspoken mystery behind the words someone is saying. It's rarely obvious. But it's there, beneath the surface of fear, anger, or resistance.

Someone who seems closed off might be asking themselves, "Am I still safe in this changing world?" Someone who lashes out might be standing at the threshold of "Do I matter anymore?"

And someone who insists they're right might be asking, silently, "If I'm wrong, what does that make me?"

In any of the scenarios above, that someone could be you. And just like anyone else, your own Threshold Question (if you have one), might be something you've clung to for ages out of survival or self-preservation.

The practice is to listen for the question beneath the conflict and to step into the unknown. It's in the unknown where you or the person you're in dialogue with can offer a story as a companion. When we meet people, including ourselves, at the threshold of fear, we become co-authors of what happens next.

YOUR MIC CHECK

Pause and take inventory of the conflicts you're carrying right now. Some may be global, like the wars that dominate headlines, injustices happening in the streets, or climate crises that redraw our maps. But others may be closer, sometimes unbearably so. Think fractured relationships with family members, a long-time friendship eroded by betrayal, a workplace disagreement that's turned into a cold war of silence.

It's worth noticing the stories we carry into conflict, not just the facts or the positions we defend, but the quieter narratives we've built about ourselves, others, or about what resolution is supposed to look like. Some stories leave room for coexistence. Others narrow the field until only winning or losing seem possible.

Sometimes that becomes clearer when we step outside of our own frame. Standing in a place like Qalandia, surrounded by people living a reality tethered by different constraints, I began to sense how many versions of endurance can exist at once, how exhaustion and resolve can live in the same body, and how everyone is holding a question, even when no one is asking it out loud.

TURN UP THE VOLUME

There's a moment in conflict when the pull to persuade becomes almost physical. You can feel it in your chest—the urge to sharpen your point in order to win the exchange. But what sits just beneath that impulse?

When someone lashes out, there's usually something they're afraid of losing. When someone digs in, they may be protecting a truth that once kept them safe. When someone refuses to listen, it's often because listening feels like a risk.

Personal stories can meet those moments differently, not as rebuttals, but as offerings. Sometimes that means naming an experience that mirrors the fear in the room. Sometimes it's admitting uncertainty. Sometimes it's letting a story sit unfinished.

This shows up in smaller moments, too—in meetings that tense without explanation and in friendships where certain topics are taboo. When someone shares something raw, the choice isn't whether to respond, but how. And when story becomes a bridge instead of a barricade, the space we coexist in widens. The stakes soften, and conversation begins to move again toward recognition.

THE DROP

Conflict will always be part of the human condition. But whether it calcifies into endless division or transforms into coexistence depends on how we navigate and narrate it.

Storytelling doesn't erase any scars. What we as storytellers can do is make sure the scars aren't the end of the story. We can identify and name every tear and every wound and set them beside someone else's to humanize the experience and heal together. This might not happen with instant harmony, but with practice we can reach alignment.

The future doesn't belong to the loudest story. It belongs to the story that makes room for opposing viewpoints. This is a story that expands rather than contracts and reminds us that even in conflict, we are standing on shared ground.

12

BREAKING THE BUBBLE: HOW TO ESCAPE ECHO CHAMBERS AND RECLAIM OUR SHARED HUMANITY (AI, ETHICS, DISINFORMATION)

I often wonder if the time I spend online is making my world smaller. On Instagram, every time I post about climate action, justice, or storytelling, like applause from the concert hall, the likes and comments stack up with nods from people who already agree with me. On LinkedIn, the same pattern plays out. My feed serves me articles from outlets I already trust and posts from colleagues who think and talk like I do. It feels good, like connection. But is it connection or just confirmation?

The algorithms know me too well. They learn my language, my network, and my preferences, and then feed me more of the same until it feels like the entire internet agrees with me. But it doesn't, and what a relief. What a breath of fresh air it is to know that my own little curated slice of reality, trimmed down to what makes me comfortable, is just that: my own small corner of the world wide web, not the world itself.

Because after a while, even the comfort that comes with confirmation can start to feel stale. Minus the dopamine hits, confirmation bias isn't actually exciting or expansive. It's predictable. Don't get me wrong. Sharing moments of solidarity with people online is an important part of modern culture. I've built up the larger part of my career on this, so dare I say that perhaps this makes me part of the problem.

As discussed in chapter 9, the algorithmic theater of outrage and applause we see online plays on a loop. It's often the same plot with slightly different headlines. One day it's a political scandal, the next it's a celebrity feud, the next it's a culture-war skirmish. But the arc is identical. It goes spark, outrage, pile-on, repeat. It's like listening to a playlist that only has three songs. At first it feels familiar. Then it becomes noise. It grows into an echo chamber we can't escape unless we unplug and move to the woods.

I keep scrolling because the feed never ends. But deep down the repetition is numbing. The world shrinks with every cycle until it starts to feel like all I have left are the same refrains, echoing back at me, while everything unfamiliar gets edited out.

I know the feeling that comes with online affirmation all too well. And chances are, if you're reading this, you do, too. You're scrolling through your feed and everything feels . . . right. The posts line up with what you already believe. Your friends are sharing articles that echo your opinions. The headlines reflect your worldview. It's cozy. It feels safe.

But safety in that sense is a trap. Comfort is a luxury when it comes to bridging divides. The problem with comfort zones, especially the ones we build online, is that they shrink our vision. They trap us in a cycle of reinforcement, preventing us from seeing the fuller picture. They block out perspectives that could stretch us. And in doing so, they make polarization worse online and in real life.

It's not simply a matter of getting along. If we're serious about repairing the divides in the US (and beyond), we have to step past our echo chambers. Staying inside them only deepens misunderstanding. And right now, those misunderstandings are tearing at the fabric of our society.

So why does stepping out matter? Because comfort zones aren't real. They're programmed. If I only engage with people who already agree with me, I'm living in a world built on my own biases and assumptions, not reality. And the truth is, people—even those whose politics I find difficult or painful—are not monolithic. Everyone has a story, a reason behind their beliefs, often rooted in personal experiences I'd never encounter inside my own bubble. When I stay comfortable, I miss those stories. And when I miss those stories, I miss connection.

When we don't challenge our own biases, we stay locked in *us vs. them*. We can't see past the caricatures, so we keep painting entire groups with one brush. That's why stepping out is vital. Doing this humanizes the other side(s). It makes us realize that even when someone's views feel alien, they're still human. They have their own fears, their own dreams, and ultimately their own reasons. Recognizing that is the first step toward understanding, reconciliation, and possibly finding common ground.

ZOOMING OUT

People have been naming this online dynamic for years. Eli Pariser called it *the filter bubble* more than a decade ago.[84] It's like an invisible editing of the internet, where personalization engines quietly trim away what doesn't fit our profile, until it feels like the entire web is nodding along in agreement.

Zeynep Tufekci has written about how that logic curates our preferences, as well as accelerates them, pushing us toward more extreme content because outrage and novelty keep us hooked longer.[85] And Pew Research has put numbers to the intuition so many of us carry.[86] Americans are sorting into information silos, trusting different outlets, and encountering fewer perspectives that cut across political or cultural lines. The issue isn't simply that we disagree on solutions. Increasingly, we're starting from different sets of facts.

The consequences of that design are everywhere. You can see them in the growth of QAnon, which functioned less like a conspiracy theory than a self-sealing loop with every contradiction reinterpreted as proof and every attempt at debunking absorbed as further evidence of the plot.[87] You can see them in WhatsApp rumors in India, where recycled clips and miscaptioned videos spread through

---

[84] Eli Pariser, *The Filter Bubble: What the Internet Is Hiding from You* (Penguin Press, 2011).

[85] Zeynep Tufekci, *Twitter and Tear Gas: The Power and Fragility of Networked Protest* (Yale University Press, 2017).

[86] Amy Mitchell, et al., "Political Polarization & Media Habits," Pew Research Center, October 21, 2014, https://www.pewresearch.org/journalism/2014/10/21/political-polarization-media-habits/.

[87] Adrienne LaFrance, "The Prophecies of Q." *The Atlantic*, June 2020. https://www.theatlantic.com/magazine/archive/2020/06/qanon-nothing-can-stop-what-is-coming/610567/.

encrypted family and neighborhood groups, fueling mob violence because they arrived stamped with the social proof of a cousin or neighbor.[88] You can see them on TikTok, where a "For You" page can learn your fascinations and your fears in hours, building corridors of content so narrow that curiosity quickly becomes confinement.[89] Even outside politics, Spotify and Netflix run on the same logic of "we're giving you *more like this, more of the same*." The result is that our playlists and watchlists expand our entertainment options, while narrowing our cultural horizons.

And now, the problem is being supercharged by artificial intelligence (AI). We've moved from "fake news" to fake everything, including faces that never existed, speeches no one gave, and fake evidence with better lighting than most documentaries.

During the 2024 election cycle alone, AI-generated robocalls and synthetic campaign videos blurred the line between persuasion and deception. In October 2025, the *Financial Times* reported that governments, political groups, and bad actors worldwide are experimenting with generative tools to flood social platforms with false images and manufactured news, creating a volume of misinformation that outpaces human fact-checkers entirely.[90]

We've moved from passive personalization to hyper-personalization. This includes feeds so finely tuned they feel intimate,

---

[88] Chinmayi Arun, "On WhatsApp, Rumours, and Lynchings," *Economic & Political Weekly* 53, no. 6 (2018), https://www.epw.in/journal/2019/6/insight/whatsapp-rumours-and-lynchings.html.

[89] "How TikTok recommends videos #ForYou," TikTok Newsroom, June18,2020.https://newsroom.tiktok.com/how-tiktok-recommends-videos-for-you?lang=en.

[90] Cristina Criddle, "Steve Bannon and Meghan Markle among 800 Public Figures Calling for AI 'Superintelligence' Ban," *Financial Times*, October 25, 2025, https://www.ft.com/content/d8bdd05d-f7aa-42ae-b880-5bbfc3a6ddb4.

while quietly stripping away friction, the very friction that helps us grow. Large language models learn from our collective online corpus—the brilliance and bias and the compassion and cruelty. The risk lives in the fact that they're feeding us back our skews in ever more polished packaging. In other words, the tools we're building are never neutral. They inherit our blind spots. And without intervention, they amplify them literally as fast as a ChatGBT or Claude AI response.

BREAKING THE LOOP

So the question now is, if the feed is built to shrink us, how do we push back? How do we keep the walls from closing in?

One way is to deliberately widen the doors of what we let enter. Maybe this looks like following people and organizations who don't sound like us, not to argue or doomscroll, but to remind us that there are other ways of seeing the same world. Sometimes this feels uncomfortable. And that's the point. Growth doesn't happen when we're wrapped in confirmation bias comfort.

Another practice is to treat news like a diet. If I only eat from one food group, my body gets weaker. If I only read from one outlet or one ideological stream, my mind does, too. Mixing left and right, mainstream and independent, global and local doesn't mean I agree with everything I consume. It means I give myself a fuller picture of the terrain. Sometimes it even means realizing I was wrong—which is humbling, and healthy.

And then there's the oldest practice of all: conversation that happens off the screen. This can take place anywhere—a town hall, a community meeting, a book club where people read current events instead of novels. Face-to-face exchanges stretch us in ways scrolling never can. Online, it's easy to reduce someone to an avatar or an argument. Offline, you see the whole person: the hesitation before they speak, the way their voice shakes or steadies, the layers behind their opinion. This doesn't guarantee agreement, but it can build the kind of empathy that algorithms can't manufacture.

Equally important is stepping away from the outrage machine. Anger sells and flare-ups keep us scrolling. As addictive as it is, most of us know that living in constant adrenaline isn't sustainable.

Therein lies the power of choice. If a post exists only to trigger rage, you can mute it. If an account profits from perpetual division, you can unfollow. The goal isn't to numb ourselves to hard truths. It's to resist the cheap manipulation of content designed to inflame rather than inform.

The tools that enable us to follow, read, and gather are simple, but the discipline is not. It requires asking, "Am I being stretched, or just soothed? Am I learning or only looping?" Breaking the bubble doesn't require us abandoning our identity or convictions. It simply means refusing to let algorithms edit the world down to a single story.

YOUR MIC CHECK

Before you scroll, it can help to pause and ask a few questions:

- Am I choosing familiarity or curiosity right now?
- Does this feed widen my view, or simply reassure it?
- When was the last time I sat with a perspective that didn't mirror my own?
- Am I confusing agreement with connection?

These aren't tests of virtue. They're small moments of awareness. Platforms are designed to reward recognition—to show us more of what already feels right, familiar, and affirming. There's comfort in that, and comfort has its place. You're a hard working human who by all means deserves comfort.

But over time, repetition can minimize our imaginations. When our consumption habits consist of echo after echo, difference starts to register as disruption rather than information. We can maintain communication and shared values with others, while inviting perspectives and stories that differ from our own.

TURN UP THE VOLUME

Escaping the echo chamber is a practice. Like building any skill, it requires repetition, discomfort, and intention.

We can start with our feeds by adding friction on purpose. I've done this, and full disclosure, I found it profoundly unpleasant. Seeing social media posts projecting views that differed so drastically from my own felt jarring at times. The impulse to dismiss them was real. And then I noticed how quickly my body wanted relief more than my brain wanted to seek common ground with the new accounts I was following.

That discomfort was an alarm signal. It told me I'd reached the edge of what I usually allowed myself to see or hear. From there, the experiment stopped being about how I felt and became more about how willing I was to pause long enough to consider a different view before reacting.

Think of your information intake the way you think about nourishment. A single source can sustain you for a while, but over time it diminishes what your system knows how to process. Exposure and range matter because understanding grows when we can recognize how the same event is told from different angles. The risk isn't disagreement. It's saturation.

This is where discernment becomes a practice rather than a rule. It means noticing what you reach for and why. It means choosing when to step back from voices that inflame without illuminating and when to stay present with perspectives that challenge you without erasing your values.

These choices may feel small. But over time, they shape what kind of public life becomes possible. Culture is built through repeated patterns of attention.

THE DROP

Breaking the cycle of spark, outrage, pile-on, repeat requires the courage to admit when our views are narrowing, the humility to seek out unfamiliar voices, and the patience to stay with the discomfort that comes from hearing stories that don't align with our own.

Our conviction is stronger when it can hold a wider view. We don't have to let technology trick us into believing the world is smaller than it is. We have a choice. And despite what we've been taught to believe about profile growth and online traction, your choice and your voice carry more weight than any algorithm designed to predict you.

In this era of companies constantly taking our data and attention, it's hard to believe that we're not as programmable as the systems built to track us. But we're not. We weren't born to passively consume whatever is thrown at us or whatever feels comfortable. We were put on this planet to create.

You're a creator. You're a storyteller. You're the writer, the producer, the director, and the star of your own movie. Every time you widen the lens, you reclaim more agency over how you move through the world. You have morals, judgment, and intuition. These are capacities no algorithm can replicate. And as much as it might seem like attention is just a commodity being taken from you, it's something you still have the power to actively direct. Where you place it determines what gains momentum, what fades, and what becomes possible next.

The future won't be decided by algorithms. It will be molded by how willing we are to stay curious, creative, and embrace our role as listeners and storytellers. That's how we stay larger than the loop and how the possibility of shared ground lives.

13

ARTIFICIAL INTELLIGENCE AND CONSCIOUS INTELLIGENCE

It was March 2019, a blizzarding day in the Austrian Alps with the kind of snow that turns even the bravest skiers into second-guessers. I wasn't there to ski. I'd had too many accidents several years prior that left me embarrassingly scooting on my butt down the black diamonds of Mammoth Mountain.

So on this snowy mountain top, I was inside drinking hot cocoa, surrounded by enterprise tech executives and brand leaders trying not to slip off the slope of digital irrelevance. They spoke fluently about data, cloud migration, and SaaS—software as a service.

I'd been hired to program the creativity and culture track of the gathering, a nod to the human side of digital transformation. After a day of panels, we traded our laptops for lanterns and hiked through a narrow, ice-cold cave toward a small hidden church carved into the mountain at St. Anton. The air smelled like stone and old prayers.

And that's where I first heard Manoj Saxena speak about the importance of creating ethical AI.[91]

Years earlier, he had led IBM's Watson division. Now, he was building what he called a global coalition of governments and private companies to pledge responsibility before AI innovation raced too far ahead. His tone carried both precision and urgency. He warned that the next war would be an AI war, not fought by giant robots but by technologies the size of flies, capable of infiltrating systems and taking them down. He spoke about the danger of AI built without ethics. Ultimately, his message was that we'd better learn to soundly govern AI or else.

I didn't realize then that I was already brushing up against a different kind of conflict, one that wouldn't fade with the news cycle because it was being built into the digital tools we rely on. I was learning about what could happen—the good, the bad, and the ugly—when human values are translated into code and when design choices begin to dictate what millions of people see, trust, and believe.

At the time, even though AI wasn't consumer-facing the way it is today, its influence was already moving outward in our smartphones and our homes. The question wasn't whether or not these systems would impact culture, but how subtly, and how fast. What I didn't yet understand was how easily these tools could be used to bend information just enough to make it feel true.

* * *

[91] Manoj Saxena, Keynote remarks on AI governance and ethics. *Digital Transformation Leadership Summit*, St. Anton, Austria, March 2019.

THE NEXT FRONT LINE

The information war didn't end when we learned to spot fake headlines. It evolved.

Once, disinformation primarily traveled through words. Now, more than ever, it flows through moving images, stories that look true before we have time to question them.

That's where Sora entered the picture. In early 2025, the generative video model created by OpenAI was still in beta, a quiet experiment that turned written prompts into film-like scenes.[92] The early clips were rough and showed images like fingers multiplying mid-gesture or shadows moving out of sync with the bodies that cast them. But even with their imperfections, they carried a strange conviction. It wasn't real, but it *felt* close.

By the fall, Sora had grown from experiment to ecosystem. OpenAI launched a social platform built around the model, allowing users to generate and share short AI-made videos in a scrolling feed. What began as a creative sandbox quickly became a new kind of social media—one where the line between storytelling and simulation was increasingly hard to see.

---

[92] Mike Issac and Eli Tan, "OpenAI's New Video App Is Jaw-dropping (for Better and Worse)," *The New York Times*, October 2, 2025. https://www.nytimes.com/2025/10/02/technology/openai-sora-video-app.html.

Geoff Brumfiel, "Kiss reality goodbye: AI-generated social media has arrived," *NPR*, October 3, 2025, https://www.npr.org/2025/10/03/nx-s1-5560200/openai-sora-social-media.

Tiffany Hsu, et al., "OpenAI's Sora Makes Disinformation Extremely Easy and Extremely Real," *New York Times*, October 3, 2025, https://www.nytimes.com/2025/10/03/technology/sora-openai-video-disinformation.html.

Around the same time, Meta introduced *Vibes*, a feed of short-form AI-generated videos inside its Meta AI app—endless, scrollable clips created from prompts and remixed by users. It looked harmless enough, filled with quick scenes, auto-generated moods, algorithmic atmospheres.

Not long after, an AI-generated character named Tilly Norwood began drawing attention online.[93] Created by the digital studio Particle6, in collaboration with Xicoia, Tilly appeared in interviews, posted on social platforms, and blurred the line between performer and program. Her expressions were polished, her presence carefully engineered. She seemed human enough to hold attention, synthetic enough to unsettle it.

Whether Vibes or Tilly came first hardly mattered. Together, they marked a turning point—the moment when our screens stopped reflecting the world and started replacing it.

Here's the troubling part for me. The same systems that can generate a face can generate faith. The same code that builds connection can just as easily counterfeit it.

Misinformation doesn't always announce itself. It feels familiar. It arrives in the cadence of a trusted voice, the lighting of a real place, and the syntax of sincerity. It's not always conveyed in a way that's trying to convince someone of something. It's designed to feel true enough to share without a second thought.

We scroll through hundreds of small fabrications a day, such as clips too perfect to question or quotes too aligned with our own

[93] Kyndall Cunningham, "The AI-generated actress that has Hollywood panicking," *Vox*, October 4, 2025, https://www.vox.com/culture/463825/tilly-norwood-hollywood-ai-generated-actress-sag-meta-openai.

biases to doubt. The danger isn't only that we'll start believing every lie. It's that we start believing less in everything else.

AI AND THE ENVIRONMENT

The rise of artificial intelligence isn't happening in the cloud. It's happening in warehouses—vast, humming data centers packed with servers that run so hot they need rivers of water and megawatts of electricity just to stay alive. Every image generated, every query processed, every simulation trained has a cost measured in compute power and carbon.

Training one large AI model can emit as much carbon as five cars over their lifetimes. Cooling systems pull millions of gallons of water from local supplies.[94] In some regions, these centers draw more power than entire towns. The invisible infrastructure of "intelligence" runs on the visible extraction of energy, minerals, and labor.

In Canada, Microsoft's expanding AI operations are already straining hydroelectric resources and pushing grid capacity to its limits.[95] Communities near new data center projects report rising energy prices and local water concerns. Across the United States, AI's electricity demand is projected to triple by the end of the decade—a spike so sharp utilities are delaying clean-energy transitions to keep up.

[94] Adam Zewe, "Explained: Generative AI's Environmental Impact," *Massachusetts Institute of Technology News Office*, January 17, 2025, https://news.mit.edu/2025/explained-generative-ai-environmental-impact-0117.

[95] Rachel Kitchin, "Microsoft's AI Boom Is a Climate Threat Canada Can't Ignore," *Canada's National Observer*, September 30, 2025, https://www.nationalobserver.com/2025/09/30/opinion/microsoft-ai-environmental-impact.

This is the paradox of progress. The same tools promising to optimize energy use and accelerate climate solutions are themselves contributing to environmental degradation. The faster we scale, the more power we burn. The more power we burn, the less credible our climate commitments become.

But this doesn't have to be the story's ending. The emissions curve of AI isn't fixed; it's a design choice. Data centers can run on solar, wind, or geothermal power. Cooling systems can recycle gray water instead of draining freshwater. Hardware can be repurposed, recycled, or redesigned for efficiency. Governments can set renewable energy mandates for AI infrastructure and enforce transparency on corporate carbon footprints.

Clean energy partnerships are already proving possible. Google and Amazon are investing in renewable-powered data campuses. Microsoft has pledged to be carbon negative by 2030—though that goal will depend on how fast their AI expansion grows. Startups are designing chips that consume a fraction of the energy used by today's GPUs, the high-powered graphics processing units that train and run modern AI systems. Engineers are experimenting with submersion cooling and modular data centers that minimize waste.

But systemic change requires more than technical fixes. It demands a cultural shift in how we define innovation—not as limitless acceleration, but as intelligent restraint. Building smarter systems means building cleaner ones. Powering intelligence should never come at the expense of the planet that sustains it.

We have an opportunity to ensure that every story about technological brilliance includes the ecosystems and communities that make it possible.

THE MUSE AND THE MACHINE

AI may influence the future, but the story guiding it still belongs to us.

The same systems that feed on data also feed on human direction—on what we reward, question, and refuse to normalize. If the environmental cost of technology is a mirror, it reflects something deeper about our attention, as well as where we place it, who we trust with it, and what we allow it to fuel.

When Manoj Saxena warned that AI needed moral frameworks, he wasn't talking only about government regulation or industry codes of conduct. He was pointing to something deeper—the human baseline of values and vision that every technology inherits from its creators.

"AI is neither good nor evil," says Kate Crawford, senior principal researcher at Microsoft and author of *Atlas of AI*.[96] "It reflects the priorities of the institutions and individuals who build it." In other words, intelligence at scale doesn't erase bias or ego; it amplifies them.

At the Climate Mic Drop event I produced in New York in 2025, Tibet Sprague, Director of Technology at Hylo, reminded the audience that even the design of technology—what it's intended to do and how it functions—is inherently tied to morality and ethics.[97] Every feature and design choice reflects a judgment about what is good or harmful, cooperative or extractive.

---

[96] Kate Crawford, *Atlas of AI: Power, Politics, and the Planetary Costs of Artificial Intelligence* (Yale University Press, 2021).

[97] Tibet Sprague, *Climate Mic Drop: Story Power in a Changing World*, Climate Week NYC, September 23, 2025, https://www.indigenousclimateaction.com/events/climate-mic-drop-story-power-in-a-changing-world.

That perspective reframes the entire debate. If every interface teaches us something about how to relate—to each other, to time, to truth—then design isn't just a technical discipline. It's cultural architecture. In the same vein, when profit is tied to engagement, outrage and addiction become intentional design features.

A social feed optimizes for immediacy, not reflection. A recommendation engine rewards repetition over discovery. A generative model learns to mimic, not to understand. These systems aren't mirrors of human behavior; they're editors of it.

That's why moral architecture must extend beyond ethics committees and corporate pledges. It has to be built into the design process itself, meaning in the defaults, the incentives, and the materials we choose to power intelligence.

As Timnit Gebru, founder of the Distributed AI Research Institute (DAIR), has argued, the real challenge with modern AI isn't whether machines become sentient; it's who controls these systems, what data they're trained on, and whose perspectives are left out of that process.[98]

So perhaps morality isn't something to be installed in machines. It's something we rebuild in ourselves and in the systems we design to reflect who we are.

AI doesn't just consume data; it consumes direction. It learns from our choices. The environmental cost of technology, the psychological toll of misinformation, and the erosion of trust all mirror a deeper truth about human attention. We are the algorithm behind the algorithm.

---

[98] Timnit Gebru, "For truly ethical AI, its research must be independent from big tech," *The Guardian*, December 6, 2021, https://www.theguardian.com/commentisfree/2021/dec/06/google-silicon-valley-ai-timnit-gebru.

Our ability to govern technology begins with our ability to govern our own focus and to write our own story.

YOUR MIC CHECK

The question isn't whether or not AI will impact our lives. It already does. The question is how consciously we participate in its influence.

These days, sometimes the line between thinking and being guided gets thin. AI tools in our email appear and offer to finish sentences for us, whether we want them to or not. AI-powered recommendations nudge us toward familiar choices for products, art, accommodations, music, and even who to date—pushing convenience center stage, wearing the costume of intuition. AI slop—low-quality, low-effort, AI-generated digital content that exploits algorithms for clicks, engagement, and monetization—is everywhere. AI is also changing how information rises to the top. Search functions now favor what's easy to reproduce and quick to rank, flooding results with content optimized for visibility rather than insight.

The effect isn't always obvious. Most of the time it feels like ease, like things working as they should. Answers appear quickly. Choices feel obvious. The path of least resistance starts to feel like your own preference.

But over time, that ease can blur where your thinking ends and where the system begins in small, almost unnoticeable ways—in a narrowing of options that reinforce what we're already used to or believe.

Sound familiar? AI is creating more echo chambers.

TURN UP THE VOLUME

If AI is learning to speak in our voice, the question becomes whether we're still willing to speak for ourselves.

There's a difference between assistance and authorship and between inspiration and substitution. When tools offer to finish our thoughts, the work becomes noticing when we accept the shortcut and when we choose to keep thinking instead.

This is an invitation to stay awake inside the technology that is consuming us—to notice when friction disappears and ask whether something vital to our creative process disappeared with it. Creativity often lives in that friction, in the uncertainty, in the sentence that takes longer to form because it wasn't generated by a machine.

Turn up the volume by choosing moments of deliberate authorship. Write the sentence yourself, even if it's messier. Ask the question before the answer appears. Sit with the half-formed idea instead of optimizing it away.

Imagination is a muscle, and it weakens when we stop exercising it.

Innovation, human-driven stories, and the future don't arrive fully formed. They're developed in the moments we decide to think, rather than default.

THE DROP

While AI companies race to show the world what else AI can do, we the people—the consumers, the creators and storytellers—need to ask what we're willing to hand over, because this kind of delegation is seductive. It promises ease, and it offers relief from having to decide, to sit with ambiguity, or author our own meaning.

As our authorship begins to slip away, what remains is synthetic substitution. Is that the worst thing? To some, absolutely. To others, not so much. Time and money are being saved, after all. But if it's at the cost of shrinking our imaginations and putting us on autopilot, we're at the risk of living in a new kind of prison, where originality has no value and freedom of expression starts getting taxed.

We can't outpace the tools we've built, but we can stay present enough to know when we're thinking for ourselves and when something else is thinking for us. And maybe that's part of the moral architecture Manoj Saxena was talking about back on that mountain in Austria. Maybe our strongest foundation is the courage to build intelligence that amplifies our keenest instincts, not our worst, the wisdom to turn power into responsibility, and the awareness to see that every story we create ourselves is a small act of governance.

The next frontier isn't only artificial intelligence. It's conscious intelligence, and it starts with us.

14

TO THE FUTURE: IMAGINATION AND WORLD-BUILDING

I've spent most of my life searching for stories, sprinting toward the next crisis or revelation with a camera, a notebook, and a microphone in hand. I thought the only way to find meaning was through motion. But somewhere between airports and a drawer full of chargers from places I could no longer place on a map, I started to lose my breath. The future didn't need me to run faster. It needed me to stand still long enough to listen.

Stillness breeds clarity. It's what remains when the noise drops. It creates the space that allows us to come home to ourselves. When I finally learned to be still, I began to see the design beneath everything I'd been following, including communities, protests, and circles of artists, survivors, and builders. All of them were doing the same essential work of imagining ways to live beyond collapse. This is a kind of world-building.

World-building may seem like fantasy on the surface. But it's more than that. It's what people do when they decide to live in a story strong enough to hold them. I've seen it in the aftermath of storms and earthquakes, when neighbors turn parking lots into relief hubs before any agency arrives. I've seen it in refugee camps where poets become recordkeepers, and in streets where murals appear overnight, transforming heartbreak into belonging.

Each of these moments holds a blueprint for survival. When we tell stories with intention, we aren't just describing the world. We're manifesting how it could be different.

Throughout all my travels, the most transformative people I met weren't necessarily the ones with the most power, funding, or reach. They were the individuals who could see a different pattern inside the same broken system and invite others to reimagine it with them. They were a farmer replanting after drought, a teacher rebuilding trust in a fractured classroom, a filmmaker refusing to frame a community through its pain and trauma alone. They didn't wait for permission to create a new world; they began sketching it in the margins of the old one.

Storytelling can loosen the grip of inevitability, and remind us that everything we inherit was once imagined, and therefore can be reimagined. Governments, economies, borders, technology—none of them arrived preordained. Someone described them first. Someone convinced others to believe.

Story is our oldest design software. Sometimes stories are artifacts—things to uncover, document, and display. But they're also the building blocks for possibility. Every time we narrate who we are, what's important to us, and where we're going, we lay another brick. That's why we need to build a foundation that can hold us.

When I stopped running, I started to notice how imagination works like infrastructure. It connects everything from policy to poetry and from code to compassion. We don't have to choose between one or the other. The future depends on both—the emotional intelligence that makes us care and the practical intelligence that helps us act.

Imagination is a collective muscle that atrophies when we outsource it to machines or to markets. Imagination is how we draft new policies before they're written into law. Most shifts in power start much smaller than we expect, with someone dreaming of a different outcome and refusing to let it go unheard.

That's the work of this moment—to tell stories boldly human enough to outlast chaos, kind enough to create belonging, and brave enough to build the unfamiliar. Imagination, at its core, is an act of faith in what is still becoming.

THE NEXT COLLABORATOR

Faith in the still-becoming asks us to look not only at what we create, but how we create it and who gets to participate in that act.

The next collaborators aren't limited to people. They're the systems, the tools, the stories, and the forces we invite to build alongside us. Some are mechanical. Some are ecological. Some are spiritual. Some are still emerging, forming their own language in the spaces where art, code, and conscience meet.

AI is only one of them, an evolving mirror of our collective behavior. It gathers what we've said, what we've shared, what we've rewarded, and reflects it back with astonishing speed. But it's not alone. Algorithms, economies, supply chains, climate systems—all of these are co-authors of the world we inhabit. Every design carries a voice. Every pattern teaches us something about what we value.

A vital part of this process is to notice what these collaborators are teaching us. Technology teaches us precision. Nature teaches us patience. Community teaches us repair. Each asks a different question about what it means to live responsibly with what we make.

I've seen people treat collaboration as an act of listening. Consider a scientist working with a river to understand its pulse before restoration, or an architect designing houses that breathe with the wind, or artists who refuse to extract a story from a place until they've learned how its people want it to be remembered. Collaboration at its highest form is reciprocity.

The tools we create—digital, mechanical, biological—are not replacements for imagination. They are invitations to refine it.

What makes creation human is self-awareness. It's knowing that every choice leaves a trace. The future of storytelling depends on how awake we remain within the worlds we're co-creating whether that's with machines, nature, or one another.

When I think about the future of story, I don't picture headlines or holograms or a hundred new AI platforms. I imagine a circle of people gathered around a shared source of light—a campfire, a stage, a screen, a protest, a classroom—listening for something that helps them feel less alone.

That impulse hasn't changed in thousands of years. What has changed are the conditions around it including the pace, the reach, and the noise. But the essence of storytelling remains the same. It's an ancient technology for remembering how to belong.

Stories regenerate the same way ecosystems do: through exchange. One person exhales an idea; another inhales it and builds. Each listener becomes a carrier of the next version. Meaning multiplies through relationship.

That's why the health of any culture can be measured by the diversity of its storytellers. A monoculture of stories leads to exhaustion—the same plots, the same heroes, the same mistakes. Regenerative storytelling restores dimensionality. It makes room for new narratives to root where old ones have decayed.

Stillness taught me that regeneration begins inside. You can't build a new world if you've lost your connection to yourself. You can't tell stories that heal if you're running on fumes. Creative acts like writing, filming, organizing, and simply dreaming are how we remind ourselves that we're part of something still alive.

STORYTELLING AS REGENERATION

Regeneration begins where exhaustion ends, because stories that sustain us are not born from speed. They rise from attention, from staying close to what aches until it reveals what it's trying to teach. Every community I've spent time in—from the aftermath of hurricanes to the desert tents where people rebuild their lives—has shown me that regeneration begins with attention. To regenerate is to keep choosing life in the presence of loss. It's the slow, deliberate work of transforming scarcity into connection.

Stories do that. They metabolize what would otherwise stay heavy. They turn isolation into language and language into belonging. When we share stories, we circulate energy the way an ecosystem recycles what falls to the forest floor.

That, to me, is the real power of story, reminding us that life continues through exchange and through listening long enough to restore balance.

WORLD-BUILDING IN PRACTICE

You can see this kind of regeneration in the stories that redefined entire landscapes of imagination.

When film director Ryan Coogler made *Black Panther*, he built a nation that had never been colonized—an African utopia grounded in ritual, science, and self-determination.[99] Wakanda was a counter-narrative to centuries of erasure. For a generation of viewers, it reframed what Black excellence, innovation, and leadership could look like. Economists cited it in conversations about African sovereignty. Educators used it to teach design thinking rooted in identity. Artists drew from its visual language to reimagine fashion, architecture, and community power. Through this movie, Coogler staged a thought experiment about liberation.

When film director Denis Villeneuve brought *Arrival* to the screen, he gave us a movie about first contact that was also a meditation on language and empathy.[100] The film asked audiences to consider communication not as persuasion or dominance, but as patient coexistence—a nonlinear exchange that resists the urgency to win. In the years that followed, scholars of diplomacy and conflict resolution referenced the film as a useful metaphor for cross-cultural listening and strategic restraint. Its central idea—that expanding how we understand another's timeline can transform our own—entered policy and academic conversations as a cultural shorthand for a more reflective approach to negotiation.

And decades before either of those films, author Octavia Butler was already sketching a future that feels closer to prophecy than fiction.

---

[99] *Black Panther*, Ryan Coogler, dir., Marvel Studios, 2018.

[100] *Arrival*, Denis Villeneuve, dir., Paramount Pictures, 2016.

In *Parable of the Sower*, she wrote about a young woman navigating the collapse of climate, governance, and faith, building a belief system called Earthseed: "God is Change."[101] Her words have since resurfaced in mutual aid networks, climate justice campaigns, and social movements that quote her verses like scripture. Through imagining a different world, Butler handed us instructions for surviving this one.

You can trace that same regenerative instinct far beyond books and film. Architects who design flood-resilient housing in Bangladesh, game designers who create immersive worlds that teach cooperation instead of conquest, and Indigenous cartographers mapping sacred sites to restore ecological memory practice world-building through their craft.

World-building, in this sense, is a rehearsal of sorts. It's how culture trains for its next evolution. Every imagined city, every alternate history, and every speculative future begin as an experiment in empathy, asking, *What would it feel like to live here? And who else could thrive if we did?*

Storytellers who build worlds are doing more than simply predicting the future. They're prototyping it.

* * *

THE RETURN TO THE STORYTELLER

In my early days as a journalist, I came into storytelling through ambition. But underneath was always awe. I was enchanted with the way so many gifted storytellers could write a song or a book or a film

[101] Octavia E. Butler, *Parable of the Sower* (Four Walls Eight Windows, 1993).

that could make pain bearable, the untouchable approachable, and the unforgivable understandable. It's always felt like alchemy.

Through writing this book, I've learned that every story I told was also mapping something within me. Each encounter, conversation, and moment of witnessing revealed another layer of what it means to pay attention and to love my life.

Stillness deepened that understanding. It reminded me that stories aren't built from urgency; they're built from presence. They live in the space between observation, curiosity, and the willingness to listen without rushing to resolve.

The people who've taught me the most—the organizers, founders, scientists, artists, and elders—carry that same patience. They understand that creation is always initially an act of listening and that the best stories make space for this.

I now see storytelling less as a craft and more as a form of stewardship. Every time someone shares a piece of their life, they're trusting you with something fragile and unfinished. We're privileged to have the chance to protect it and allow it to change us.

Stories alone can't save us, but they can light our way back to one another and to what we love and cherish most about this life.

YOUR MIC CHECK

Every story begins with a glimmer of awareness. You know the feeling. It happens the moment you realize you have something to say and that you might want the world to hear it. It's small at first, almost shy. Then it gathers weight.

This is you taking inventory of why you're speaking and what the cost might be. Before a word leaves your mouth, there's a current running through you, possibly in the form of memory, conviction, doubt, or love. Everything you've lived is threaded through that current. Every teacher, every witness, every silence that once felt unbearable.

To check your mic is to remember that nothing you create exists in isolation. Every voice is a continuation of other voices. You are part of that chain. When you speak, those voices travel with you.

Language can be a form of compassion, a weapon, or a bridge. That's what the mic check is for—to find steadiness before sound and to remember that authenticity, once released, can't be recalled.

When you finally speak, let it be from that place—the one that doesn't need to be right, only real.

TURN UP THE VOLUME

When a story leaves your hands, it doesn't end. It travels across rooms, timelines, and people you'll never meet. It's altered by every listener, adjusted by every retelling, carried into places you've never been.

We live in an age where attention is currency and distortion is cheap. But the deeper current—the one that keeps culture alive—still moves through honesty, empathy, and risk.

To turn up the volume is to let a story breathe beyond your own experience. It's to amplify the truths that intersect with you, the neighbor rebuilding what was lost, the scientist fighting to turn evidence into action, the child asking why the world is burning and still full of wonder.

Volume is continuity. It's the thread that keeps stories from being buried. It's how one person's courage becomes another's permission. It's the chain reaction that turns voice into movement.

When you turn up the volume, let it be for that reason—to connect what's been separated and to help meaning travel further than the moment it was born.

THE DROP

There's a moment after every mic drop when the noise fades and resonance replaces sound. The meaning of the performance lingers in the air, waiting for someone else to breathe it in and make it their own.

There's a transition between the space of what's been spoken and what's still becoming. This kind of evolution is rarely graceful. It hums before it harmonizes. It stumbles before it sings. But that's how new worlds begin, through friction, faith, and persistence.

It's up to us to make sure that no machine, government, or algorithm decides how the next chapter reads. It can be written by us through the stories we refuse to silence, the communities we choose to build, and the questions we keep alive.

When it's your turn at the mic, remember to have grace for yourself. To speak your mind about the current state of the world is to make a bold statement.

Your voice and your stories are a gift. They can steady someone on the edge of giving up or spark the first draft of a new policy. They move through the world in ways you may never witness with the power to build new worlds.

Thank you for being with me as I shared my stories about this one.

Now go grab the mic with both hands—and remember to pass it on.

EPILOGUE

The first time I raced through Hollywood, I was chasing stories that belonged to other people—celebrities, visionaries, the already-amplified. Later, I raced through the Middle East, running after stories that belonged to entire nations. But it was through bearing witness to and writing stories about conflict, coexistence, and creation that I learned about what storytelling can truly do for others.

After years of travel, deadlines, and emotional avoidance, I came home to Michigan to rest and be present. My dad was sick but light-hearted as always. While the thought of staying still in my hometown was foreign and unsettling, the possibility of being overseas and getting a phone call in the middle of the night that he passed was not an option.

Between hospital visits and long walks along the river with my dog, I began to write to try to make sense of the different lives I've lived so far. In those months, the noise of the world faded long enough for a signal to come through. The stories I had collected from film sets, award ceremonies, Wall Street, and the edges of war zones rearranged themselves into a map I could follow, reminding me that we are all, in our own ways, trying to be heard before we're gone.

My father passed away before I finished writing this book, but his quiet presence before his last few days with us supported the breath of every page. He loved books. He loved stories, whether they came from National Geographic, rows of science fiction novels, or the newspaper. For him, stories seemed to be about a return to peace, a return to self. Writing this book was my return.

What I've learned most from this writing process is the value of presence and the beauty of being imperfectly human. I've also learned that a story is not a destination. It's a rhythm for us to keep creating and dancing to anytime, anywhere.

This book may be close to ending, but the deeper story—the one you're living—continues. All of the questions you've asked, from the heartbreaking and heart-opening realizations you've uncovered to the silences you've begun to fill, are not closing acts. They are thresholds.

You know what it means to own your narrative, to share it with intention, and to hold the stories of others with integrity. You've traced how stories seed relationships, movements, and legacies, and how they inform culture and the chemistry of connection.

Most importantly, I hope that at some point while reading this book, you've remembered that you're not alone. Your story is part of a constellation. Every time you speak your truth, reframe an inherited narrative, or help someone else step into the light of their own story, you find a frequency for someone else.

The future needs your voice—not the refined and polished version—the honest one. It needs your courage and your creative vision. It needs your imagination, as radical as it is grounded, as fierce as it is tender.

So if you're waiting for permission to tell your story, consider this it.

If you're waiting for the perfect time, the perfect idea, the perfect medium—it doesn't exist.

Start with where you are. Start with what you know. Start with what your body remembers and what your heart won't let go of, and trust that your story, when told with integrity, can do more than just move someone. It can move the world.

So, storyteller,

Pick up the thread again.

Step into the circle.

Write, speak, film, paint, code, or sing your story.

Tell it messy. Tell it raw. Just tell it.

Your story is part of a larger weave, a tapestry that holds us all. When you dare to share it, you change the course of what's possible.

So begin right here, right now.

The mic is yours.

RESOURCES

"About the Project." Humanizing Deportation. University of California, Davis. Accessed November 15, 2025. https://humanizandoladeportacion.ucdavis.edu/en/about-the-project/.

"ACJP Holds First Ever Mitigation Packet Workshop for Families." *Albert Cobarrubias Justice Report*. AC Justice Project. November 10, 2024. https://acjusticeproject.org/2014/11/19/acjp-holds-first-ever-mitigation-packet-workshop-for-families/.

"Airbnb.org expands temporary housing support for refugees." Airbnb Newsroom. June 20, 2024. https://news.airbnb.com/airbnb-org-expands-temporary-housing-support-for-refugees/.

"Apple's Tim Cook says he's proud to be gay." *The Express Tribune*. October 14, 2024. https://tribune.com.pk/story/783541/apples-tim-cook-says-proud-to-be-gay.

Arun, Chinmayi. "On WhatsApp, Rumours, and Lynchings." *Economic & Political Weekly*, 53, no. 6 (2018). https://www.epw.in/journal/2019/6/insight/whatsapp-rumours-and-lynchings.html.

Batista, Ed. "Antonio Damasio on Emotion and Reason." *Ed Batista Executive Coach blog*, July 31, 2011. https://edbatista.com/2011/07/antonio-damasio-on-emotion-and-reason.html.

Bendick, Eric, director. *The Path of the Panther.* National Geographic, 2023.

Betts, Alexander and Paul Collier. *Refuge: Transforming a broken refugee system*. Penguin Books, 2017.

Brown, Roger and James Kulik. "Flashbulb memories." *Cognition*, 5, no. 1 (1977): 73–99. https://doi.org/10.1016/0010-0277(77)90018-X.

Brumfiel, Geoff. "Kiss reality goodbye: AI-generated social media has arrived." *NPR*, October 3, 2025. https://www.npr.org/2025/10/03/nx-s1-5560200/openai-sora-social-media.

Bruneau, Emile G. and Rebecca Saxe. "The power of being heard: The benefits of 'perspective-giving' in the context of intergroup conflict." *Journal of Experimental Social Psychology*, 48, no. 4 (2012): 855–866. https://doi.org/10.1016/j.jesp.2012.02.017.

Buolamwini, Joy. *Algorithmic Justice: Race, Bias, and Power in the Age of AI.* Random House, forthcoming 2025.

Butler, Octavia E. *Parable of the Sower.* Four Walls Eight Windows, 1993.

Cahill, Larry and James L. McGaugh. "Mechanisms of emotional arousal and lasting declarative memory." *Trends in Neurosciences*, 21, no. 7 (1998): 294–299. https://doi.org/10.1016/S0166-2236(97)01214-9.

Casey, Michael. "Appeals Court Rules Trump Administration Can End Legal Protections for More than 400,000 Migrants." *The Associated Press.* September 12, 2025. https://apnews.com/article/ef3eb9ff1a2728fadc2f76f865086b2c.

Chatterji, Aaron "Ronnie" and Michael W. Toffel. "The New CEO Activists." *Harvard Business Review.* January–February 2018. https://hbr.org/2018/01/the-new-ceo-activists.

Chira, Susan and Catrin Einhorn. "How tough is it to change a culture of harassment? Ask the women of Ford." *New York Times.* December 19, 2017. https://www.nytimes.com/interactive/2017/12/19/us/ford-chicago-sexual-harassment.html.

Chung, Andrew. "US Supreme Court Backs Trump on Aggressive Immigration Raids." *Reuters.* September 8, 2025. https://www.reuters.com/world/us/us-supreme-court-backs-trump-aggressive-immigration-raids-2025-09-08/.

"City of Cape Town—2011 Census Suburb Nyanga." Strategic Development Information and City of Cape Town. July 2013. https://resource.capetown.gov.za/documentcentre/Documents/Maps%20and%20statistics/2011_Census_CT_Suburb_Nyanga_Profile.pdf.

Coleman, Alistair. "Ukraine conflict: Further false images shared online." *BBC News.* February 25, 2022. https://www.bbc.com/news/60528276.

Colorado, Meiling. "Standing Rock became not just a simple protest, but a working, living example of what was possible, what could be done." *Permaculture Women's Guild.* Accessed January 14, 2026. https://www.permaculturewomen.com/standing-rock/.

"Common Claims About Proposition 13." Legislative Analyst's Office (LAO). September 19, 2016. https://lao.ca.gov/Publications/Report/3497.

"Consideration of Deferred Action for Childhood Arrivals (DACA)." US Citizenship and Immigration Services. Accessed November 15, 2025. https://www.uscis.gov/DACA#:~:text=On%20June%2015%2C%202012%2C%20the,DACA%20for%20the%20First%20Time.

Constitution of the Kingdom of Bhutan. Royal Government of Bhutan. 2008. https://www.constituteproject.org/constitution/Bhutan_2008.

Coogler, Ryan, director. *Black Panther*. Marvel Studios, 2018.

"COP28 Ends with Call to Transition Away from Fossil Fuels." *United Nations News*. December 13, 2023. https://news.un.org/en/story/2023/12/1144742.

Coto, Dánica. "Residents of Puerto Rico Can't Vote for President, but Their Anger at Trump Is Still Shaping the Race." *PBS NewsHour*. October 28, 2024. https://www.pbs.org/newshour/politics/residents-of-puerto-rico-cant-vote-for-president-but-their-anger-at-trump-is-still-shaping-the-race.

Crawford, Kate. *Atlas of AI: Power, Politics, and the Planetary Costs of Artificial Intelligence*. Yale University Press, 2021.

Criddle, Cristina. "Steve Bannon and Meghan Markle among 800 Public Figures Calling for AI 'Superintelligence' Ban." *Financial Times*. October 25, 2025. https://www.ft.com/content/d8bdd05d-f7aa-42ae-b880-5bbfc3a6ddb4.

Cunningham, Kyndall. "The AI-generated actress that has Hollywood panicking." *Vox*. October 4, 2025. https://www.vox.com/culture/463825/tilly-norwood-hollywood-ai-generated-actress-sag-meta-openai.

Damasio, Antonio. *Descartes' Error: Emotion, Reason and the Human Brain*. Penguin, 2005.

DiNapoli, Jessica and Jonathon Stempel. "Ben & Jerry's accuses Unilever of muzzling it because of Trump." *Reuters*. January 27, 2025. https://www.reuters.com/legal/ben-jerrys-accuses-unilever-muzzling-it-because-trump-2025-01-24.

DiNapoli, Jessica. "Ben & Jerry's calls war in Gaza a 'genocide.'" *Reuters.* May 29, 2025. https://www.reuters.com/world/middle-east/unilevers-ben-jerrys-calls-war-gaza-genocide-2025-05-29.

DiNapoli, Jessica. "Ben & Jerry's says parent Unilever silenced it over Gaza stance." *Reuters.* November 14, 2024. https://www.reuters.com/business/retail-consumer/ben-jerrys-says-parent-unilever-silenced-it-over-gaza-stance-2024-11-14.

Dougherty, Dale. "Place C: Crisis mode for COVID-19." *Make: Magazine.* March 30, 2020. https://makezine.com/article/maker-news/plan-c-crisis-mode-for-covid-19/.

"Dreamers' Stories." Durban.Senate.gov. Accessed November 15, 2025. https://www.durbin.senate.gov/issues/immigration-and-the-dream-act/dreamers-stories.

Elcin, Zillah. "Meeting the moment: Freedom of the Press Foundation's 2024 Impact Report." Freedom of the Press Foundation. February 12, 2025. https://freedom.press/about/announcements/2024-impact report/.

"Empowerment through employment for Syrian refugee women in Jordan." *UN Women News.* August 10, 2018. https://www.unwomen.org/en/news/stories/2018/8/feature-empowerment-through-employment-for-syrian-refugee-women-in-jordan.

"Equity vs Equality: Where It Differs (And How to Embrace Justice)." Embracing Equity. December 11, 2025. https://www.embracingequity.org/post/equity-vs-equality-where-it-differs-and-how-to-embrace-justice.

"Facebook's systems promoted violence against Rohingya; Meta owes reparations." *Amnesty International.* September 29, 2022. https://www.amnesty.org/en/latest/news/2022/09/myanmar-facebooks-systems-promoted-violence-against-rohingya-meta-owes-reparations-new-report/.

"Fact Sheet: Expanded Expedited Removal." *National Immigration Forum*. May 14, 2025. https://forumtogether.org/article/fact-sheet-expanded-expedited-removal/.

Fashion Revolution. Accessed November 15, 2025. https://www.fashionrevolution.org/about/.

Foundation for Individual Rights and Expression (FIRE). Accessed October 2025. https://www.thefire.org.

Friedersdorf, Connor. "Overcaffeinated on the Starbucks 'Race Together' Campaign." *The Atlantic*. March 18, 2015. https://www.theatlantic.com/business/archive/2015/03/overcaffeinated-attacks-on-the-starbucks-race-together-campaign/388072/.

Gebru, Timnit. "For truly ethical AI, its research must be independent from big tech." *The Guardian*. December 6, 2021. https://www.theguardian.com/commentisfree/2021/dec/06/google-silicon-valley-ai-timnit-gebru.

"George Floyd protests: Misleading images and videos that have been shared on social media." *BBC Bitesize*. Accessed December 15, 2026. https://www.bbc.co.uk/bitesize/articles/zwjqcmn.

Gonzalez Bocinski, Sarah. "Time for Solutions." *Futures Without Violence blog*. May 15, 2018. https://futureswithoutviolence.org/news/time-for-solutions-summit.

Hasson, Uri, Asif A. Ghazanfar, Bruno Galantucci, Simon Garrod, and Christian Keysers. "Brain-to-brain coupling: A mechanism for creating and sharing a social world." *Trends in Cognitive Sciences*, 16, no. 2 (2012): 114–121. https://doi.org/10.1016/j.tics.2011.12.007.

Hillberry, Russell and Manuel I. Jimenez. "The Effect of the Jones Act on Puerto Rico." *Research Briefs in Economic Policy*, No. 380. CATO Institute. April 2024. https://www.cato.org/research-briefs-economic-policy/effect-jones-act-puerto-rico.

Hines, Kevin. *Cracked, Not Broken: Surviving and Thriving After a Suicide Attempt*. Rowman & Littlefield Publishers, 2013.

"History of Adoption in Korea." Korean Adoption Services. Accessed November 15, 2025. https://www.kadoption.or.kr/en/info/info_history.jsp.

"Housing Justice Narrative Toolkit." PolicyLink. Accessed October 2025. https://www.policylink.org/sites/plorg/files/2025-07/Policylink_Housing_Justice_Toolkit_2-13.pdf.

"How TikTok recommends videos #ForYou." TikTok Newsroom. June 18, 2020. https://newsroom.tiktok.com/how-tiktok-recommends-videos-for-you?lang=en.

Hsu, Tiffany, Stuart A. Thompson, and Steven Lee Myers. "OpenAI's Sora Makes Disinformation Extremely Easy and Extremely Real." *New York Times*. October 3, 2025. https://www.nytimes.com/2025/10/03/technology/sora-openai-video-disinformation.html.

Human Right to Water (HR2W) Portal. State Resources Control Board. California Water Boards. Accessed January 14, 2026. https://www.waterboards.ca.gov/water_issues/programs/hr2w/.

"India lynchings: WhatsApp sets new rules after mob killings." *BBC*. July 20, 2018. https://www.bbc.com/news/world-asia-india-44897714.

"Introducing Vibes: A New Feed of AI Videos at the Center of Meta AI." Meta Newsroom. September 2025. https://about.fb.com/news/2025/09/introducing-vibes-ai-videos.

Issac, Mike and Eli Tan. "OpenAI's New Video App Is Jaw-dropping (for Better and Worse)." *The New York Times*. October 2, 2025. https://www.nytimes.com/2025/10/02/technology/openai-sora-video-app.html.

Joyful Heart Foundation. https://www.joyfulheartfoundation.org/about-us/our-mission/.

Jung, Carl. *Man and His Symbols*. Aldus Books, 1964.

Kapoor Kanupriya. "Conservation body calls for global moratorium on deep-sea mining." *Reuters*. September 8, 2021. https://www.reuters.com/business/environment/conservation-body-calls-global-moratorium-deep-sea-mining-2021-09-09/.

Keown, Damien, editor. "Rinpoche." *Oxford Dictionary of Buddhism*. Oxford University Press, 2013.

Kirby, Jen. "The impossible task of truth and reconciliation." *Vox*. March 24, 2022. https://www.vox.com/22979953/forgiveness-reconciliation-truth.

Kitchin, Rachel. "Microsoft's AI Boom Is a Climate Threat Canada Can't Ignore." *Canada's National Observer*. September 30, 2025. https://www.nationalobserver.com/2025/09/30/opinion/microsoft-ai-environmental-impact.

Kozman, Claudia, Rana Tabarra, and Jad Melki. "The Role of Media and Communication in Reducing Uncertainty During the Syria War." *Media and Communication* 9, no. 4 (2021): 297–308. https://doi.org/10.17645/mac.v9i4.4352.

LaFrance, Adrienne. "The Prophecies of Q." *The Atlantic*. June 2020. https://www.theatlantic.com/magazine/archive/2020/06/qanon-nothing-can-stop-what-is-coming/610567/.

Larson, Jonathan. "La Vie Bohème." *Rent*, 1996.

"Later Is Too Late: Impact Report." Time for Better. February 7, 2024. https://timeforbetter.org/wp-content/uploads/2024/02/TimeforBetter-LaterisTooLate-ImpactReport24-004o-NOLOGO.pdf.

Li, Xinyu. "Quantifying the Economic Impact of 2025 ICE Raids on California's Agricultural Industry: A Case Study of Oxnard." Cornell University (submitted August 5, 2025). https://doi.org/10.48550/arXiv.2508.03787.

Lieberman, Matthew D., Naomi I. Eisenberger, Molly J. Crockett, Sabrina M. Tom, Jennifer H. Pfeifer, and Baldwin M. Way. "Putting feelings into words." *Psychological Science*, 18, no. 5 (2007): 421–428. https://doi.org/10.1111/j.1467-9280.2007.01916.x.

"Made in Za'atari: Women Refugee Entrepreneurs Make Their Mark." Blumont International. October 23, 2023. https://blumont.org/project/made-in-zaatari/.

"Managing the COVID-19 infodemic: Promoting healthy behaviours and mitigating the harm from misinformation and disinformation." World Health Organization. September 23, 2020. https://www.who.int/news/item/23-09-2020-managing-the-covid-19-infodemic-promoting-healthy-behaviours-and-mitigating-the-harm-from-misinformation-and-disinformation.

McGaugh, James L. "The amygdala modulates the consolidation of memories of emotionally arousing experiences." *Annual Review of Neuroscience*, 27 (2004): 1–28. https://doi.org/10.1146/annurev.neuro.27.070203.144157.

Mehta Angeli. "Policy Watch: After fraught global meeting, future of deep-sea mining still hangs in balance." *Reuters*. Updated August 4, 2023. https://www.reuters.com/sustainability/policy-watch-after-fraught-global-meeting-future-deep-sea-mining-still-hangs-2023-08-03/.

Melimopoulos, Elizabeth. "Trump announces Israel-Hamas ceasefire deal: What we know and what's next." *Aljazeera*. October 9, 2025. https://www.aljazeera.com/news/2025/10/9/trumpannounces-gaza-ceasefire-deal-what-we-know-and-whats-next.

Million Voters Project. Accessed October 2025. https://www.millionvotersproject.org.

Mitchell, Amy, Jeffrey Gottfried, Jocelyn Kiley, and Katerina Eva Matsa. "Political Polarization & Media Habits." Pew Research Center. October 21, 2014. https://www.pewresearch.org/journalism/2014/10/21/political-polarization-media-habits/.

Narrative 4. Accessed November 22, 2025. https://narrative4.com/about-n4/.

"Narrative Change." Freedom for Immigrants. Accessed November 15, 2025. https://www.freedomforimmigrants.org/narrative-change.

Narrative Initiative. Accessed October 2025. https://www.narrativeinitiative.org.

Nobel, Carmen. "When CEOs Become Activists." *Working Knowledge*. Harvard Business School. April 20, 2016. https://www.library.hbs.edu/working-knowledge/when-ceos-become-activists.

Pariser, Eli. *The Filter Bubble: What the Internet Is Hiding from You*. Penguin Press, 2011.

"PayGas Plans to Install 52 Pay-as-you-Gas Stations in SA." *Clean Cooking Alliance*, July 14, 2020. https://cleancooking.org/news/07-14-2020-paygas-plans-to-install-52-pay-as-you-gas-stations-in-sa/.

Pennebaker, James W. "Writing about emotional experiences as a therapeutic process." *Psychological Science*, 8, no. 3 (1997): 162–166. https://doi.org/10.1111/j.1467-9280.1997.tb00403.x.

Pennebaker, James W. and Beall, S. K. "Confronting a traumatic event: Toward an understanding of inhibition and disease." *Journal of Abnormal Psychology*, 95, no. 3 (1986): 274–281. https://doi.org/10.1037/0021-843X.95.3.274.

Pennebaker, James W. and Joshua Smyth. *Opening Up by Writing It Down: How Expressive Writing Improves Health and Eases Emotional Pain* (3rd ed.). Guilford Press, 2016.

Pflum, Mary. "A year ago, Alyssa Milano started a conversation about #MeToo. These women replied." *NBC News.* October 15, 2018. https://www.nbcnews.com/news/us-news/year-ago-alyssa-milano-started-conversation-about-metoo-these-women-n920246.

Phelps, Elizabeth A. "Human emotion and memory: interactions of the amygdala and hippocampal complex." *Current Opinion in Neurobiology*, 14, no. 2 (2004): 198–202. https://doi.org/10.1016/j.conb.2004.03.015.

Ramasubramanian, Madhuri, Divya Patel, Megan R. Turner, and Vincent Ybarra. "The influence of life narrative themes on resilience and life outcomes." *Personality and Individual Differences*, 185, (2022): 111235. https://doi.org/10.1016/j.paid.2021.111235.

"Ramallah." *Britannica.* October 23, 2025. https://www.britannica.com/place/Ramallah.

Rawabi official website. Accessed November 22, 2025. https://rawabi.ps/.

"Reframing Early Childhood Development and Learning." *Core Story Brief.* FrameWorks Institute. Accessed October 2025. https://www.frameworksinstitute.org/app/uploads/2020/03/reframingearlychilddevelopment_alamancecounty.pdf.

Reid, Helen. "Google, BMW, AB Volvo, Samsung back environmental call for pause on deep-sea mining." *Reuters.* Updated March 31, 2021. https://www.reuters.com/business/sustainable-business/google-bmw-volvo-samsung-sdi-sign-up-wwf-call-temporary-ban-deep-sea-mining-2021-03-31/.

Reid, Tim, Sebastian Rocandio, Pilar Olivares, and Leah Douglas. "Immigration Raids Leave Crops Unharvested, California Farms at Risk." *Reuters*. June 30, 2025. https://www.reuters.com/business/immigration-raids-leave-crops-unharvested-california-farms-risk-2025-06-30/.

"Report of the Independent International Commission of Inquiry on the Occupied Palestinian Territory, Including East Jerusalem, and Israel (A/HRC/56/26)." Human Rights Council. United Nations. May 27, 2024. https://www.un.org/unispal/document/coi-report-a-hrc-56-26-27may24/.

Rowley, Melissa Jun. "Building a Culture of Courage and Accountability this Sexual Assault Awareness Month and Beyond." *Rolling Stone*. Culture Council. April 15, 2025. https://www.rollingstone.com/culture-council/articles/building-courage-accountability-sexual-assault-awareness-beyond-1235317002/.

Rowley Melissa Jun. "Comment: For Indigenous peoples, failure to increase biodiversity finance is a matter of life or death." *Reuters*. December 5, 2024. https://www.reuters.com/sustainability/society-equity/comment-indigenous-peoples-failure-increase-biodiversity-finance-is-matter-life-2024-12-05/.

Rowley, Melissa Jun. "How This Family of Founders Is Working to Make Puerto Rico More Self-Sufficient through Local Farming & Delivery." *Forbes*. April 26, 2020. https://www.forbes.com/sites/melissarowley/2020/04/26/how-this-family-of-founders-is--working-to-make-puerto-rico-more-self-sufficient-through-local-farming--delivery/.

Rowley, Melissa Jun. "Meet the Entrepreneur Who Started the First Pharmaceutical Company Owned by Women of Color in the US." *Forbes*. December 31, 2021. https://www.forbes.com/sites/melissarowley/2021/12/31/meet-the-entrepreneur-who-started-the-first-pharmaceutical-company-owned-by-women-of-color-in-the-us/.

Rowley, Melissa Jun. "Trailblazers of Puerto Rico: Meet the Couple Making Shields for Healthcare Workers on the Frontlines of COVID-19." *Forbes*. April 11, 2020. https://www.forbes.com/sites/melissarowley/2020/04/10/trailblazers-of-puerto-rico-meet-the-couple-making-shields-for-healthcare-workers-on-the-front-lines-of-covid-19/.

Rowley, Melissa Jun. "What Silicon Valley Can Learn from Lebanon's Women in Tech." *TechCrunch*. June 6, 2017. https://techcrunch.com/2017/06/06/what-silicon-valley-can-learn-from-lebanons-women-in-tech.

Rowley, Melissa Jun. "Women of Puerto Rico Unite to Bring Justice to Victims of Domestic Violence & Sexual Assault." *Forbes*. May 12, 2021. https://www.forbes.com/sites/melissarowley/2021/05/12/women-of-puerto-rico-unite-to-bring-justice-to-victims-of-domestic-violence--sexual-assault/.

Sanzum, Tausif. "New Video Series Maps Stories of Immigrants' Journeys to the US." American Friends Service Committee. 25 July 2025. https://afsc.org/newsroom/new-video-series-maps-stories-immigrants-journeys-us.

Saxena, Manoj. Keynote remarks on AI governance and ethics. *Digital Transformation Leadership Summit*. St. Anton, Austria. March 2019.

"Schools and Communities First Campaign." California Calls: Building Power for Working-Class Communities. Accessed October 2025. https://www.cacalls.org.

"Shaping Tomorrow: Time for Better's Impact on COP28's 'Later Is Too Late' Campaign." Time for Better. Accessed October 2025. https://timeforbetter.org/agency-news/shaping-tomorrow-time-forbetters-impact-cop28s-lateristoolate-campaign.

"Sixteenth meeting of the Conference of the Parties to the Convention on Biological Diversity (COP 16)." Convention on Biological Diversity. Updated February 27, 2025. https://www.cbd.int/conferences/2024.

Speri, Alice. "More than 1,000 US students punished over speech since 2020, report finds." *The Guardian*. May 15, 2025. https://www.theguardian.com/us-news/2025/may/15/us-students-campus-speech.

Sprague, Tibet. *Climate Mic Drop: Story Power in a Changing World*. Climate Week NYC, September 23, 2025. https://www.indigenousclimateaction.com/events/climate-mic-drop-story-power-in-a-changing-world.

Stening, Tanner. "Can Puerto Ricans Vote in the Presidential Election? What Role Do US Territories Play in Elections?" *Northeastern Global News*. October 28, 2024. https://news.northeastern.edu/2024/10/28/can-puerto-ricans-vote-presidential-election/.

StoryCorps. Accessed November 22, 2025. https://storycorps.org/about/.

Stuart, Hunter. "Waze Lets Israelis Avoid Palestinian Areas, but Not the Other Way Around." *VICE Magazine*. October 5, 2016. https://www.vice.com/en/article/waze-lets-jewish-israelis-avoid-palestinian-areas-but-not-the-other-way-around/.

"Suicide Deterrent Net: Saving Lives at the Golden Gate Bridge." Golden Gate Bridge, Highway and Transportation District. Accessed October 20, 2025. https://www.goldengate.org/district/district-projects/suicide-deterrent-net/.

"Syria profile—Timeline." *BBC News*. January 14, 2019. https://www.bbc.com/news/world-middle-east-14703995.

Tech2Peace. Accessed November 22, 2025. https://www.tech2peace.com/.

The People's Supper. Accessed November 22, 2025. https://thepeoplessupper.org/.

Tong-Hyung, Kim and Claire Galofaro. "Adoption Fraud Separated Generations of South Korean Children from Their Families, AP Finds." *PBS Frontline*. September 14, 2024. https://www.pbs.org/wgbh/frontline/article/korean-children-adoption-fraud/.

Trimmel, Suzanne. "Nearly 200 Percent Surge in School Book Bans During 2023–2024 School Year." Pen America. November 1, 2024. https://pen.org/press-release/nearly-200-percent-surge-in-school-book-bans-during-2023-2024-school-year/.

Truby, John. *The Anatomy of Story: 22 Steps to Becoming a Master Storyteller*. Faber & Faber, 2007.

Tufekci, Zeynep. *Twitter and Tear Gas: The Power and Fragility of Networked Protest*. Yale University Press, 2017.

Tutu, Desmond and Britannica Editors. "Truth and Reconciliation Commission, South Africa." *Britannica*. Updated September 29, 2025. https://www.britannica.com/topic/Truth-and-Reconciliation-Commission-South-Africa.

United Nations Office for the Coordination of Humanitarian Affairs (OCHA) in the Occupied Palestinian Territory. Accessed November 22, 2025. https://www.ochaopt.org.

Untapped Global. Accessed September 12, 2025. https://untapped-global.com.

Ura, Karma and Karma Galay. *Gross National Happiness and Development: Proceedings of the First International Seminar on Operationalization of Gross National Happiness*. Centre for Bhutan Studies, 2004. See speech by Jigme Singye Wangchuck: "Gross National Happiness," 1972.

Ura, Karma, Sabina Alkire, Tshokie Zangmo, and Karma Wangdi. *An Extensive Analysis of GNH Index.* Centre for Bhutan Studies and GNH Research, 2012.

Villeneuve, Denis, director. *Arrival.* Paramount Pictures, 2016.

"Vision, Values, Voice: A Communications Toolkit." Opportunity Agenda. Accessed October 2025. https://opportunityagenda.org/our-tools/communications-toolkit/.

Vivo Alliance. https://www.vivoalliance.org.

Vosoughi, Soroush, Deb Roy, and Sinon Aral. "The spread of true and false news online." *Science,* 359, no. 6380 (2018): 1146–1151. https://doi.org/10.1126/science.aap9559.

Youn, Soo. "Nike sales booming after Colin Kaepernick ad, invalidating critics." *ABC News.* December 21, 2018. https://abcnews.go.com/Business/nike-sales-booming-kaepernick-ad-invalidating-critics/story?id=59957137.

"Yara Yassin." Creative Ind MENA. Accessed November 15, 2025. https://creativeindmena.com/speaker/yara-yassin/.

"Yes on Prop 15: Schools & Communities First Campaign." Power California. Accessed October 2025. https://powercalifornia.org/scf.

"Za'atari Camp Factsheet." *United Nations High Commissioner for Refugees.* December 2024. https://reliefweb.int/attachments/ea753d3e-b643-484a-a033-40c6fb5144cc/Zaatari%20Fact%20Sheet_December%202024.pdf.

Zewe, Adam. "Explained: Generative AI's Environmental Impact." *Massachusetts Institute of Technology News Office,* January 17, 2025. https://news.mit.edu/2025/explained-generative-ai-environmental-impact-0117.

ABOUT THE AUTHOR

Melissa Jun Rowley is a seasoned media and tech entrepreneur, communications strategist, and global climate justice advocate with more than two decades of experience developing and executing narratives at the intersection of social innovation and the evolving media landscape. A former CNN and Associated Press Television News producer and BBC News contributor, Melissa has covered everything from entrepreneurship in conflict regions and war zones to start-up hubs in Africa to First Amendment infringements in the US, bringing visibility to underreported stories that challenge dominant narratives and inspire action.

She has written for *Reuters, Rolling Stone, CBS News, The Guardian, Fast Company, TechCrunch, Forbes*, and *National Geographic*, exploring the convergence of climate justice, culture, and storytelling. Melissa is also the founder and producer of Climate Mic Drop, a global summit and storytelling platform convening artists, activists, Indigenous leaders, investors, and policymakers to reimagine how narrative drives climate solutions and systemic change. A sought-after international speaker, she regularly presents at the world's most influential convenings, including Davos, SXSW, Web Summit, the UN Climate Conference (COP), New York Climate Week, LA Climate Week, San Francisco Climate Week, DC Climate Week, the Hollywood Climate Summit, the Climate Leadership Conference, Sundance Film Festival, Cannes Film Festival, and the United Nations General Assembly. Her talks explore how story—not just data—moves policy, bridges divides, and builds coalitions for lasting change.

As the founder and CEO of Warrior Love Productions, she created communications strategies and high-impact campaigns to accelerate decarbonization, elevate gender equity, and drive environmental justice. She has consulted on marketing strategy for the UN Climate Change Global Innovation Hub, the World Bank, Cisco, KPMG, MasterCard, William Morris Endeavor, and several high-growth scale-ups and mission-driven nonprofits.

She currently leads communications for REVERB, the leading force greening the music industry through partnering with artists such as Billie Eilish, FINNEAS, Harry Styles, Dave Matthews Band, Dead & Company, Jack Johnson, and Lorde to decarbonize live shows at the source, make tours more sustainable, and engage fans with the climate and social justice initiatives these artists care about most.

Previously, while working with legendary musician and activist Peter Gabriel, Melissa co-founded *The Toolbox*—a humanitarian platform providing mentorship and digital tools for social entrepreneurs in developing economies. While living across the UK, Europe, the Caribbean, the Middle East and North Africa, she wrote extensively about women founders for *ForbesWomen*, highlighting what the US can learn from the resilience and ingenuity of women-led ventures abroad.

She is also an advisor for Women and Climate and Creatives for Climate, a UN Media for Impact Award recipient, and a Founder Institute alumnus. At her core, Melissa believes in storytelling not just as an art, but as an act of faith in humanity, solidarity, and system-shifting truth.

HIRE MELISSA TO SPEAK

Melissa Jun Rowley has addressed audiences of thousands around the world on storytelling, narrative equity, climate justice, and leadership in public-facing institutions.

Her work includes keynote addresses and high-profile moderations at global convenings such as the World Economic Forum, COP, Web Summit SXSW, the Cannes Film Festival, the Sundance Film Festival, and gatherings connected to the United Nations General Assembly, and global Climate Weeks.

Drawing on her background as a former journalist, media entrepreneur, and founder of Climate Mic Drop, Melissa connects culture, policy, and imagination with precision and context—supporting conversations that extend beyond the stage.

To inquire about booking Melissa for your next conference, summit, or leadership gathering:

☞ melissajunrowley.com
🖂 mel.rowley@gmail.com

The B Corp Movement

Dear reader,

Thank you for reading this book and joining the Publish Your Purpose community! You are joining a special group of people who aim to make the world a better place.

What's Publish Your Purpose About?

Our mission is to elevate the voices often excluded from traditional publishing. We intentionally seek out authors and storytellers with diverse backgrounds, life experiences, and unique perspectives to publish books that will make an impact in the world.

Beyond our books, we are focused on tangible, action-based change. As a woman- and LGBTQ+-owned company, we are committed to reducing inequality, lowering levels of poverty, creating a healthier environment, building stronger communities, and creating high-quality jobs with dignity and purpose.

As a Certified B Corporation, we use business as a force for good. We join a community of mission-driven companies building a more equitable, inclusive, and sustainable global economy. B Corporations must meet high standards of transparency, social and environmental performance, and accountability as determined by the nonprofit B Lab. The certification process is rigorous and ongoing (with a recertification requirement every three years).

How Do We Do This?

We intentionally partner with socially and economically disadvantaged businesses that meet our sustainability goals. We embrace and encourage our authors and employee's differences in race, age, color, disability, ethnicity, family or marital status, gender identity or expression, language, national origin, physical and mental ability, political affiliation, religion, sexual orientation, socio-economic status, veteran status, and other characteristics that make them unique.

Community is at the heart of everything we do—from our writing and publishing programs to contributing to social enterprise nonprofits like reSET (https://www.resetco.org/) and our work in founding B Local Connecticut.

We are endlessly grateful to our authors, readers, and local community for being the driving force behind the equitable and sustainable world we are building together.

To connect with us online, or publish with us,
visit us at www.publishyourpurpose.com.

Elevating Your Voice,

Jenn T. Grace

Jenn T. Grace

Founder, Publish Your Purpose

www.ingramcontent.com/pod-product-compliance
Ingram Content Group UK Ltd.
Pitfield, Milton Keynes, MK11 3LW, UK
UKHW041827200726
13854UKWH00002BA/645

9 798887 972404